Just Say YES
by Erec Lindberg

Copyright © 2014 - All Rights Reserved

All rights reserved. No part of this publication may be reproduced, distributed, or transmitted in any form or by any means, including photocopying, recording, or other electronic or mechanical methods, without prior written permission of the publisher, except in the case of brief quotations embodied in critical reviews and certain other noncommercial uses permitted by copyright law.

DISCLAIMER: The information in this book does not substitute for medical care. Do not discontinue use of medication, or disregard the advice of your medical professional. This information is a supplement to any current health care treatment, and is not intended to diagnose or cure. Always consult your doctor. The author and publisher of this book are not responsible for the actions of the reader.

Just Say YES

EREC LINDBERG

Dedicated To
Dolores and Robert Lindberg

Whose
Thoughts, Words And Acts
Prove Beyond a Shadow of a Doubt
that Unconditional Love
Is Possible.

Table of Contents

FOREWORD 17

CHAPTER 1
WHAT IS YOUR INNER VOICE? 23

CHAPTER 2
WHERE IS YOUR INNER VOICE LOCATED? 29

CHAPTER 3
WHAT DOES YOUR INNER VOICE FEEL AND SOUND LIKE? 33

CHAPTER 4
THE TRUTH OF YOUR INNER VOICE 37

CHAPTER 5
THE IMPORTANCE OF YOUR INNER VOICE 41

CHAPTER 6
THE FREEDOM OF YOUR INNER VOICE 45

CHAPTER 7
THE POWER OF YOUR INNER VOICE 49

CHAPTER 8
THE STRENGTH OF YOUR INNER VOICE 55

CHAPTER 9
BECOMING AWARE OF YOUR INNER VOICE 61

CHAPTER 10
HEARING YOUR INNER VOICE 67

CHAPTER 11
TRUSTING YOUR INNER VOICE 71

CHAPTER 12
ACTING ON YOUR INNER VOICE 75

CHAPTER 13
LIVING WITH AND FROM YOUR INNER VOICE 79

CHAPTER 14
THE CLARITY OF YOUR INNER VOICE 85

CHAPTER 15
A PERSONAL JOURNEY WITH YOUR INNER VOICE 89

CHAPTER 16
GROWING INTO THE ENERGY OF YOUR INNER VOICE 93

CHAPTER 17
YOUR INNER VOICE AND THE FORK IN THE ROAD 97

CHAPTER 18
YOUR INNER VOICE AND THE TRAILBLAZER IN YOU 101

CHAPTER 19
YOUR INNER VOICE AND YOUR HIGHEST VISIONS... 105

CHAPTER 20
RAISING YOUR FREQUENCY THROUGH YOUR INNER VOICE 111

CHAPTER 21
YOUR INNER VOICE AND READING HIGHER FREQUENCY MATERIAL 117

CHAPTER 22
YOUR INNER VOICE AND OUTER APPEARANCES 123

CHAPTER 23
YOUR INNER VOICE AND SOMEONE ELSE'S RULES 127

CHAPTER 24
YOUR INNER VOICE IS GOD WITHIN YOU 131

CHAPTER 25
SPEAKING FROM YOUR INNER VOICE 135

CHAPTER 26
YOUR INNER VOICE IS YOUR PERSONAL GPS 139

CHAPTER 27
YOUR INNER VOICE AND LIVING IN THE ABUNDANCE FLOW 143

EPILOGUE.. 147

In Memory Of And Tribute To Jane Bishoff

My dear friend, Jane Bishoff, sadly passed away before she could hold a copy of *Just Say YES* in her hands. There are moments I can still feel her influence in its pages. Through our eleven years of friendship, Jane consistently encouraged me to listen to my *Inner Voice* and to keep writing.

In our often direct and laughter-filled conversations, she would remind me of how important it was to get the message of *Just Say YES* out into the world. She shared her personal journey and the obstacles she overcame in her early years with the help of her *Inner Voice* as it guided her through those challenges.

She truly believed that everyone should be taught how to hear, trust and act on their *Inner Voice's* guidance and that it could well be the greatest gift they might ever receive.

Jane stood in the center of the word *YES*. Whenever I hosted a community gathering her reply was always the same, "*YES* of course, Richard and I will be there," followed by, "Can we do anything to help?"

Jane and Richard, her loving husband of thirty-five years, emotionally supported me when I made the decision to sell my beloved Montana home. It wasn't long before I got the call from Jane informing me that *YES,* from now on I was to consider their home to be my *new* Montana home. She always ensured that I had a vehicle to drive on my visits, even after I mangled the front end of her SUV. I am so very grateful for those times spent with Jane and Richard.

Jane and Richard, you are a team who have always had my back. Thank you for your commitment to help me and to help others *Just-Say-Yes* to their *Inner Voices*.

Jane, you are deeply loved and greatly missed by all of us.

Special Acknowledgments

Thank you to my editor, Dace Whitney, for meeting in this lifetime and being a great support in bringing this material to completion. I hold great appreciation for your editing direction in the process of writing this book. Thank you for a terrific ride in this unfolding journey.

To my dear friend Kathy Greidanus for your generous encouragement, supportive input, and deep respect for my *Highest Visions*. You were the insightful sounding board for Dace and myself.

To Glenda Hanna for your supportive influence in my life since childhood. Thank you for your insightful proof reading and heartfelt input at the eleventh hour. Your friendship is invaluable.

From the heart center of *Who I Am* as I write in this moment, I express my love and gratitude to everyone who has supported me in the birth of this book. *Just Say YES* has benefited greatly from the wisdom and generosity of many others: Danit Almog, Claudia Alt, Jack and Lynn Anderson, Ann Bellwood, Andrea Bennet, Vivian Bridaham, Rolf Burgi, Adrianna Cohen, Tom Crisp, Patti Cuttler, Susan Ferrin, Hali Fleming, Ann Fleuchaus, Cyndi Fonda, Danielle Freeburg, Doug Freeman, Ginger Lee Frost, Coats Guiles, Sandy Johnson, Peggy Larsen, Nancy Lindberg, Deb Maccabee, Gwen Marlow, Norma Mitchell, Kimberly Errington Moers, Nola and Jerry Mosher, Bill and Linda Musser, Lisa Nicoll, Julie Petersen, Tom Newbury and Tom Sandon, Susanne Phelps, Stephanie Rivera, Susan Rockefeller, Gina Rogak, Anne-Marie Rolfe, Ardis Scott, Paul Sheenan, Celeste Simone, Lisa Tener, Joyce Van Baak, Marian Waddems, Robin Wilcox.

Also my heartfelt thanks to the late Dr. Manion, Dr. Steve Kritsick, and Mark Lindberg.

To Elizabeth Gilbert, Neale Donald Walsch and Napoleon Hill for bringing their work into the world.

Just Say YES

Foreword

*J*UST SAY YES IS a Handbook created to help you hear, trust and act on guidance from the most valuable asset you own—your *Inner Voice*. As the last frontier of unexplored *inner* wealth, it holds the power to reveal the truth about *Who You Are* and *What You Came Here To Do*.

We were never taught about our *Inner Voice* at home or in school, even if we experienced brief glimpses of it as a *gut feeling*, *hunch*, *insight* or *intuition*. We had no idea that we could rely on it to make daily choices and life-altering decisions with ease and confidence. We were unaware that it could lead us directly to our *Highest Visions*, those dreams and desires that best reflect our true Self.

Instead, we have been left to fumble through life under the false pretenses of security and unconscious to the fact that we are trapped *Above The Neck* in the chaos of our *Thinking Mind* as it plays *Connect The Dots* under the influences of the *Outer Appearances*.

Far too many people will never walk a path that is different from the herd because fighting the *Outer Appearances* would be too uncomfortable to handle. They don't trust themselves with their unique personal expression. They don't want to embarrass themselves. They do not feel strong (or supported) enough to experience the *Vast Unknown* within them, especially when the process doesn't fit *Someone Else's Rules*.

They are not brave enough to enthusiastically dig around in their passions if it means not having a job right after graduation or taking a "time-out" after they have been downsized. They fear walking the solitary path of Self (re)discovery if it means not having a relationship or partner with whom they feel safe. They have lost their personal sense of adventure and checked out. They are just going through the motions. They drop in front of the TV each night and go unconscious.

You Are Not One Of Them!

In this moment, you may feel overwhelmed like you're lost in the desert. You may feel hopeless or helpless because you can't see the light at the end of the tunnel. You may be experiencing a "dark night of the soul" moment when you no longer feel connected to the frequency of your dreams or desires.

You are not alone in these moments of despair.

Countless men and women whose names may be familiar to you have passed through these dark moments and into the light of their truth. Thomas Edison spent a great deal of time in that dark place. So did Abraham Lincoln. John Grisham lived there for some time. J.K. Rowling gave birth to Harry Potter there.

Like them, you can *choose* in this moment to hear, trust and act on your *Inner Voice's* guidance and begin to walk your unique path toward *Who You Are* and *What You Came Here To Do*. Choose to live in the *Vast Unknown* of yourself, just as they did in pursuit of their *Highest Visions*. Choose to stand firmly in a new *You* despite all *Outer Appearances*.

You will not be alone! You will have your *Inner Voice* to lead you!

Once you connect with your *Inner Voice,* you will begin to see that it does not matter what you do for a living. Rather, it is about doing the inner expansion work while you are paying the bills and keeping food on the table.

You will soon understand that it is of no consequence that you are unemployed, lost in a sea of career choices or unfulfilled in your relationship. Rather, it *IS* about trusting yourself to pursue your *Highest Visions* simply by choosing to do so in each moment. It *IS* about an inner knowing at the beginning of each day that the answers lie inside of you.

Once you connect with your *Inner Voice,* you will begin to stand in *Your Light—Who You Are* and *What You Came Here To Do*. It may take a leap of faith, as it did in my case, or perhaps a *breakdown* in order for you to *break through* your *Thinking Mind's* rigid adherence to *Outer Appearances.*

Cracking open in their individually defining *breakthrough* moments, three internationally renowned authors whom I respect have documented and shared their *Inner Voice* journeys as they followed an inner pull to reveal their truest selves. Their revelations have encouraged millions of readers to activate and begin their journeys.

In her phenomenally successful bestseller, *Eat, Pray Love*, Elizabeth Gilbert reveals that her life doesn't take off until she is lying prostrate on the bathroom floor connecting with the truest part of who she is. By *Outer Appearances* she has a good life with a successful career, loving husband, and nice home, but until this moment, she has not yet heard her *Inner Voice.*

Similarly, Neale Donald Walsch, in his *Conversations With God* series, documents the struggles in his life, relationships, and careers until he hears his *Inner Voice* begins to act on it.

Nearly a century ago, Napoleon Hill, though he has various short-lived career successes, cannot make his life work until he loses everything materially. While on an afternoon walk at the lowest point in his life, he hears his *Inner Voice* for the first time. He returns home inspired to review his years of interviews and research on a stalled project, and writes, over a three-month period, *Think And Grow Rich*, considered to be the best-selling self-help book of all time.

In *Just Say YES,* I share my breakthrough moment when I first consciously connect to my *Inner Voice* at nineteen years old while walking to math class. This and each Personal Story I share with you is designed to activate you to awaken to your *Inner Voice*. I encourage you to enjoy the process of learning to hear, trust and act on it as you become *Consciously Aware* of your personal journey that has brought you to these pages. As with Elizabeth, Neale and Napoleon, your *Inner Voice* will open *You* up to your life.

Your *Inner Voice* is REAL. It is triggering you as you read this.

You might be aware of it now, or it might surface tomorrow or even six months from now. Do not worry if you cannot feel or hear it today, it will come. Elizabeth, Neale and Napoleon are three powerful examples of this truth.

As you become more *Consciously Aware*, you will begin to hear your *Inner Voice* in different ways and feel its energy lying inside of you. You will learn to trust it as you act on its directions. Those *Highest Visions* that you begin to achieve will further validate the authenticity of its truth.

Your *Thinking Mind* will no doubt create resistance in all forms, using *Outer Appearances* to discourage the journey out of your safety zone. But know that your safety zone is nothing more than a false reality. True security lies ONLY within you!

I chose *Just Say YES* as the book title because my *Inner Voice* directed me to do so, just as it directed each step on my path as I wrote these words. Each time I found myself *Above The Neck* and trapped in the chaos of my *Thinking Mind's* resistance, I would *Just—Say—Yes* and drop *Below The Neck*, choosing instead to hear, trust and act on my *Inner Voice's* direction.

I never planned to be a writer, nor did I imagine that I could ever write persuasively enough to convey a coherent, powerful message. But my *Inner Voice* led me through the *Vast Unknown*—past self-limiting thoughts and behavior created by my *Thinking Mind*—to write these pages.

Just Say YES is intended to help you break through the chaos of your *Thinking Mind* and to bring you further into alignment with *Who You Are* and *What You Came Here To Do*.

Your *Inner Voice* will lead you on the truest path that you can walk in this state of being human. Join me in consciously choosing NOW, in this very moment, to begin to hear, trust and act on its guidance!

Chapter 1
What is Your Inner Voice?

YOUR *INNER VOICE* IS the most valuable asset you own. It speaks to you from your inner core located *Below The Neck And Above The Waist*. It is available to you 24/7 and 365 days a week. It is your best friend. Your inner guide. A powerful mentor.

Friendship with God, by Neale Donald Walsch, describes the *Inner Voice* as a 'voiceless voice' or a 'feeling with words around it.'

Think of all the times that you have had a *hunch* to act on something. An *intuition* bumping you. A *gut-feeling* that rings true. An *insight* to follow. We use these terms to describe our *Inner Voice* as it speaks to us.

This 'voiceless voice' is a *feeling connected to a thought that comes up from inside of me* in many instances. The feeling and thought have an energy that I sense. After years of honoring the process, I'm clear that the thought does not emanate from *Above The Neck* in my *Thinking Mind*. You may become aware of the feeling before you do the thought that is connected to it. Regardless, you will come to recognize this energy as it surfaces upward in you.

Sadly, the vast majority of us are not taught to recognize the *Inner Voice* in either our youth or adulthood. Yes, we may become familiar with the aforementioned terms, but there is no focused effort to develop our *Inner Voice*. We merely use those terms to describe a feeling or thought without a *Conscious Awareness* of the powerful concept that they represent. If the concept isn't taught at home, and since it isn't taught in schools, then it isn't honored as an important tool for both living and thriving in our physical world.

Too many of us actually learn to ignore it. Instead, we rely solely on what occurs *Above The Neck* in our *Thinking Mind*, remaining focused on and distracted by the drama and chaos of the *Outer Appearances* that surround us.

Thanks to the efforts of a growing number of enlightened individuals who have discovered *Who They Are* and *What They Came Here To Do*, and who have helped to raise our global human consciousness, more of us are becoming aware of *THE* most important tool we have to guide us daily as we create the lives we want.

Best-sellers, like Rhonda Byrne's 2006, *The Secret*, have raised the awareness of millions of people to the Law Of Attraction. This basic universal premise has always been an active force in our lives regardless of when (or if) we become aware of it. Only in the past century have quantum physics studies attempted to explore, understand and illuminate this powerful concept of manifestation.

Hearing, Trusting and Acting from our Inner Voice's guidance is a key component in the manifestation process.

Now is the time to harness the power of your *Inner Voice* and manifest the life you desire. *Just Say YES* recounts my personal journey over forty-two years of life-altering choices I have made by listening to, trusting and acting on my *Inner Voice's* wisdom. Through sharing my experiences, I intend to trigger within you those memories of instances when your *Inner Voice* spoke to you, regardless of whether you heard it or acted upon it at the time, and bring those memories into your *Conscious Awareness*. You'll see how you've already had years of preparation just lying there, waiting to help you bring into your life the joy, abundance and love that are the essence of *Who You Are* and *What You Came Here To Do*.

The voice inside speaks to you daily regardless of whether you are aware of it. Being unaware of your *Inner Voice* does not mean that you aren't honoring it. You may well be and not even know it. It is important to note, however, that if you aren't *Consciously Aware* of it, then you aren't fully accessing and utilizing its power as you consider and act on important decisions; especially those that can be life-altering.

Once you are *Consciously Aware* of your *Inner Voice*, trusting and acting on it from moment to moment, you will free yourself from the daily stress—even the paralyzing fear—that may otherwise hold you back from stepping into a more enriching life. Our *Inner Voice* feels (and is) directly connected to our dreams, visions, desires, and passions. These, in turn, reflect the truth of *Who We Are* and *What We Came Here To Do* in this lifetime.

You may have a sense right now as you read this that it feels important to accept these concepts as truths. That's your *Inner Voice* being triggered. You can feel the energy of it. Take a moment to consider this.

Having grown to implicitly trust my *Inner* Voice over the years, I recognize that it has helped me to create and expand my life to its fullest potential in each moment. In fact, it led me to write, *Just Say YES* to share my journey within its pages.

Personal Story
A Letter To The Landlord

On a bitter cold morning in mid February 1995 I stopped dead in my tracks halfway across my bedroom floor. A *feeling followed by a thought* had suddenly come up through me causing me to react in total fear. I stood dumbstruck as I felt my *Inner Voice* push me to write a letter to my roommate's landlord requesting a two-bedroom apartment.

"What? Oh My God the landlord doesn't even know I exist!" My name wasn't on the lease, and I wasn't even sure if I could legally share a one-bedroom NYC apartment with my roommate. My *Thinking Mind* yelled, "They'll throw you out when they find out you're living here!" I felt overwhelmed. Why would my *Inner Voice* push me do to something with an unknown outcome like this?

I had been lucky to share the ridiculously low monthly expenses on this rent-controlled apartment for several months with a friend who occupied it only eight days a month when he came into New York City for TV work. In truth, the apartment was being loaned to him by his friend, 'Texas' Tom, who had long ago moved to—you guessed it -Texas. I'd never even met the man on the lease, and now my *Inner Voice* was pushing me to write the landlord! I could jeopardize both Tom's lease and the inexpensive living accommodations for my roommate, Steve, and myself.

I felt sick to my stomach. I didn't know if I could do what I felt I knew I *NEEDED* to do inside. If only I could just skip over this day and pretend that I didn't have this feeling coming up from that place inside me that I had grown to trust—La, La, La, La, La, putting my fingers in my ears. Except then I'd be living from *Above The Neck* in my *Thinking Mind*, which I had learned years earlier was *NOT* where truth lives.

I had trusted the voice that lives *Below The Neck And Above The Waist* for years through all kinds of situations. It had always served me well, but I was momentarily filled with this *Thinking Mind*-induced fear.

I felt numb as I enclosed the letter with the monthly rent check and mailed it. All the while my *Thinking Mind* continued to scream, "Oh My God!" For days I lived in fear that I would find an eviction notice posted on the door or get a call from the landlord telling me, "Get Out!"

And yet ... nothing happened. Each month I felt my *Inner Voice* urge me to include a personal note with the rent check requesting the two-bedroom apartment for Tom (the phantom roommate on the lease whom I'd never met) and myself. I didn't dare tell either Tom or Steve about my letters to the landlord.

And then it happened. A man one floor above me who had been living in a rent-controlled, two-bedroom apartment for over thirty years suddenly died. His extended family, if any, didn't bother to empty out the apartment, so now it was in the city's jurisdiction. Tape crisscrossed the door until the matter was legally cleared up. Months passed. Then one day the tape was gone and there were workmen inside. I took a peek. It was small, but it had two bedrooms with lots of sun from a western exposure!

My *Thinking Mind* immediately took control to push me to call the landlord, overpowering my *Inner Voice* that was telling me to calmly be patient and wait. And then the landlord answered. As I began to introduce myself and ask about the apartment, she immediately cut me off, snapping, "I've received all your letters and I don't know what I am going to do with the apartment!" I sheepishly apologized for sounding pushy, and I visibly shook as I put the phone down, thinking (*Above The Neck*—again!) that I had spoiled months of *Inner Voice*-directed groundwork with her.

Several days later the phone rang. I heard the landlord's voice ask me if Tom and I were still interested in the new apartment? I said, "Yes! Yes we are!" She continued, "Someone will be right over to show it." When I told her that I'd already seen it, she cut me off insisting, "I need *YOU* to look at it with *MY* representative—right now!"

As I listened to her cold and blustery words, my *Thinking Mind* raced. "You bet! Anything you say! What would you like me to wear? Can I bring coffee? Do you like warm chocolate chip cookies 'cause I'll run get you some and send them back to you with your representative! Yes ma'am! Yes ma'am! Yes ma'am!"

Yet I heard a steady voice—my *Inner Voice*—say that of course I would be happy to meet her representative—immediately! Meanwhile, my *Thinking Mind* was in the throes of releasing months of pent up emotions. When I hung up the phone I did a jig (in place *AND* in quadruple time—not easy) yelling, "Yes! Yes! Yes!" I was dizzy with joy! And just as quickly, I struck what I thought a military stance and salute would look like. While I'm sure it wasn't anything near a West Point standard, the action did serve to calm my emotions, and I got back down *Below The Neck*. I didn't dare go back *Above The Neck* with everything that was pending.

The landlord called later that day to ask about our decision. Damn! I had not wanted to face the fact that Tom, and not I, was the current, fully vetted and approved, tenant in the building—and the one who would naturally need to sign the new lease. I stammered that Tom would not be back from Dallas until next week, (which he actually would be) but that I'd Fed-Ex the lease for his signature. She immediately replied, "I am *NOT* comfortable leasing the apartment to someone who hasn't *SEEN* the apartment." My heart immediately dropped below sea level.

Then she continued, "Here's what we can do. We'll put the lease in your name and Tom can be your roommate." Never in my wildest dreams did I imagine that I would be the only one on the lease! No vetting! That easy! *THANK YOU! THANK YOU INNER VOICE*! I had just secured the golden ticket to the chocolate factory! A rent controlled two-bedroom apartment on the Upper West side in New York City! And one block from The Park—as in Central! Thank You God!

If you haven't experienced the 'pleasure' of the journey to find an apartment—a rent-controlled one mind you—much less securing a lease in New York City, you may not truly comprehend how monumental was this moment!

As I write, I can recall years earlier my first spiritual teacher encouraging me to call forth the divine apartment, in divine scheduling at the divine price. Well let me tell you, it worked! My *Inner Voice* had consistently urged me forward as I acted on my divine intention at the beginning of every day through all these months—despite my *Thinking Mind* questioning every move.

I would not still have this lease today if it hadn't been for my *Inner Voice* pushing me to move past mountainous fear and the *Outer Appearances* telling me that I could never have what I wanted. Some years later while I was traveling for extended periods, I found a roommate whose monthly rent share (which is ideal for him) covers all of my monthly apartment expenses.

Oh, the joy of living rent-free in New York City—one block from Central Park! So much for the expression "Location! Location! Location!" The new phrase to live by in today's world is *"Inner Voice! Inner Voice! Inner Voice!"*

Manifesting What You Want In Your Life Is Directly Proportional To Hearing, Trusting And Acting On Your Inner Voice Guidance.

Chapter 2
Where Is Your Inner Voice Located?

YOUR INNER VOICE IS located Below The Neck and Above The Waist.

As you visualize this area, you will recognize that it does not include your Thinking Mind. I'm pointing out what is a very important line of division—The Neck.

The area Below The Neck is where your heart is located. When you think too much, you are nowhere near your heart. Above The Neck is too far you're your truth.

Remember the real estate rule, "Location! Location! Location!" Well this is a great rule of thumb when you consider the Inner Voice and the heart; they both lie in that region Below The Neck and Above The Waist!

Hello Lewis & Clark—where's your packhorse? Yes, you're going to be trail blazing as you explore the last frontier of You—your Inner Voice. Just—Say—Yes, take a step forward, and remember to breathe. Here we go!

You are responsible for creating everything you experience in your life. Everything! No Exceptions! This idea might be new to you and seem startling, overwhelming, and even unnerving. Let's just offer it up now as we Just—Say—Yes and put it in the shopping cart as we head to the check out.

And let's up the ante by acknowledging that up until now you have created just about everything in your life through your

Thinking Mind. You know, that area Above The Neck between your ears! Look at your life and ask yourself, "How's it workin' for ya?"

This question is a reality check reminding us that we all have areas of our lives we would like to change—areas that we don't like (anymore) or that cause us to feel unhappy and dissatisfied. Why do we continue to put up with these issues day after day, year in and year out? "How's it workin' for ya?" holds your Thinking Mind accountable for all its past choices and actions.

You will soon come to see that your Inner Voice is a powerful agent for change. It has the power to 'un-create' anything that your Thinking Mind has created. It can save you from past situations, like "What was I thinking when I bought that shirt?" to "Why did I make that commitment to be in my cousin's wedding?" to "Where was my head when I started dating so and so?" Yes, un-create all those things that you no longer want in your life.

Through your Inner Voice, you will become aware of those things you never wanted in the first place, but your Thinking Mind didn't know it at the time or based its choices on Outer Appearances that do not reflect your truth. Transitioning Below The Neck and allowing your Inner Voice to guide you forces a powerful re-direction of your life.

Because we were never taught about our Inner Voice, we have almost exclusively used our Thinking Mind (that in turn has relied on the Outer Appearances) to make our life decisions and choices. But our Thinking Mind doesn't realize that the Outer Appearances aren't real. Rather, they are just our Thinking Mind's version of reality based on its previous experiences and the belief systems it has created around them.

Just Say YES, along with your Inner Voice, will help you to become Consciously Aware of your real truth. And it has nothing to do with the Outer Appearances! Allowing your Inner Voice to lead you forward is going to make for one heck of an interesting ride as you awaken to the new You. And along the way you're going to have some fun too!

Personal Story
The Bike of My Dreams

One June day, I felt pulled to buy a mountain bike to ride around New York City. I live on Manhattan's upper west side, a block from Central Park and four blocks from a path that runs along the Hudson River. As I walked into my local bike shop, I happened to look up and discover the most beautiful bike I'd ever seen. I had never seen one like it. I heard myself gushing to the sales person about the bike's unique design and beauty, asking what it was called as well as the price. It wasn't a mountain bike. It was a road bike called a "Y Foil," made by Trek. And it had a price tag of $4,000—and that was years ago!

Since my budget was less than half of that figure, I headed for the mountain bikes. I took several brands out for test rides, always feeling numb when I looked at the Y Foil each time I returned to the shop. My Thinking Mind rationalized that I could "deal" with a non Y Foil bike, and I finally left with a (sort of) beautiful yellow "Specialized" brand mountain bike and hit the paths around the city.

Several days later while running errands, I saw a man on a Y Foil that was cobalt blue, my favorite bike color at the time. In that moment, my Inner Voice finally got the better of my Thinking Mind, wrapping it with duct tape as it pulled me back to the bike shop. I asked about the Y Foil and they said that it had just gone on sale for $2700!

My Inner Voice pushed me to immediately order the Y Foil in cobalt blue. But it also told me to wait for a couple of months to pick it up on my birthday, August 12th! I don't think I have ever experienced that level of anticipation over a period of time. It was a shock to my system!

The day was sunny and beautiful when I picked up that bike. I can't begin to describe the immense feeling of gratitude that came up inside me when I put my foot on the pedal and rode my very own cobalt blue Y Foil down the street!

Acting from inside brought a deeper level of satisfaction and joy than I had ever experienced. I love my Inner Voice for guiding me forward to claim what my Thinking Mind told me I didn't need or couldn't have.

I have never seen another cobalt blue Y Foil anywhere since I saw that one on the street that activated me to return to the bike store to find that mine was on sale. Months later while out riding, I suddenly remembered that a year earlier I had visited a friend at a sports networking event. As I was leaving, I had walked by a cobalt blue Y Foil—perhaps it was the one I later saw on the street.

There Are Moments When My* Inner Voice *Has Shown Me Ahead Of Time—If I Am Willing To Accept It—Some Blessing That Is Coming Into My Life.

Chapter 3
What Does Your Inner Voice Feel and Sound Like?

OUR *INNER VOICE* HAS many ways to attract our attention.

As a warm, welcome feeling that comes over us.

As a chill that comes up through us.

As a tingle at the back of our neck in recognition of a truth coming into our mind.

As a thought that sounds or feels true to us although we can't explain why.

As an *Inner Voice* "thought" that is 'louder' than our *Thinking Mind* "thoughts."

As a spontaneous insight spoken directly from our lips in conversation.

As a feeling/thought from outside of our *Thinking Mind* that simply appears in it.

As a gentle push that is just enough to motivate a simple action, like picking up the phone to call someone.

As a calmness that comes for several minutes, hours or days before we become aware of what we will be shown.

As a conversation between our *Inner Voice* and our *Thinking Mind*. Back and forth. Back and forth. We feel that inner dialog surface up within us.

My *Inner Voice* can be quite tenacious; at times it will not leave me alone. It runs the same sentence, picture, feeling or thought around in my consciousness until it triggers me to pay attention. Most often it must be *THAT* insistent to push my *Thinking Mind* beyond its comfort zone, like opening up to a change in circumstances or a new situation; unexpectedly changing my schedule; accepting something that I know is true for me; accepting something that my *Thinking Mind* says I can't afford or have; or accepting that I have the wisdom to actually do or achieve my *Highest Visions*, etc.

The force of my *Inner Voice* push is often directly proportional to the resistance of my *Thinking Mind* to release its perception of the *Outer Appearances*.

Personal Story
Shaving at the Sink

One day as I was shaving at my bathroom sink, up into my *Thinking Mind* came the thought of a childhood neighbor from Montana whom I had neither seen nor spoken to in fifteen years. I knew there must be a reason for her to suddenly come into my thoughts in the middle of shaving. So I walked into my office, and after five phone calls, tracked her down. She was now living in Iowa.

I told her about the inner push motivating me to call, and I asked if she was all right. She confessed that she was not, having married a man a few months earlier and then moving to Iowa for his job. She told me that she was deeply unhappy and felt trapped there with her two children (from an earlier marriage) because she had leased out her house in Washington State.

Just as my *Inner Voice* pushed me to make the initial call, it then continued to push me on a daily basis to give her support over the phone through the coming weeks. I could hear the truth of my *Inner Voice* come up from inside me during our phone conversations. These conversations, in turn, activated her inner truth to start making the necessary changes in her life.

Within a month she had left her husband, packed up and moved out of Iowa. Within three years, she was living her childhood dream, having sold her Washington State home to move back to the family farm in Montana where she was earning a good living from her home office and enjoying her life.

Honoring the feeling of my truth that came up inside while I was shaving helped a childhood friend to get back on track with her life. My *Inner Voice* continued to push me to work with her by phone all through those years of transition.

Honoring our inner guidance is not just about obtaining all the toys to which we feel attracted. It is about helping the people in our lives. If we don't honor that feeling as it comes up in us, then we cannot serve those people who are important to us. We are all here to help each other. I have written *Just Say YES* to remind you that you already know this inside.

Your *Inner Voice* carries with it a message of truth for you and for the people around you. Your *Inner Voice* knows no state lines, time zones or distances. It may speak to you at any time. It can even be heard while you shave—if you are *Consciously Aware* and willing to listen.

Living From Your* Inner Voice, *You Are A Beacon Of Light Illuminating The Truth In Others, Guiding Them Closer To Who They Are And What They Came Here To Do.

Chapter 4
The Truth of Your Inner Voice

WE HAVE FORGOTTEN WHAT is true for us.

We cannot hear or feel what is true for us.

We do not honor what is true for us even when we are aware of it.

We are conditioned to live our lives unconsciously, going through the motions and living one hundred percent from our *Thinking Minds* completely unaware of our *Inner Voice*. Even if we aren't unconscious, the stress of our hectic lifestyles keeps us from gaining a clear perspective on our truth. In most instances, we are definitely not present in the moment.

Even those of us who are conscious may refuse to face the fact that our belief systems don't seem to fit our lives. What we think we believe is more often *NOT* related to our truth.

For example, all of the states have a speed limit no higher than 75 miles per hour. Even the least expensive new car can hit that with ease. Yet we still see advertising for new high performance cars with speedometers that go to 150 mph—double the legal speed limit.

Where are we going to use that horsepower without breaking the law? Why do we think we need this much engine power? Why do we work so hard to pay for these expensive, high performance toys? We have lost touch with what is true for us in all the commercial advertising noise—the *Outer Appearances*.

I am not saying that owning one of these automobiles is wrong. I have driven several of them, but in each case I was directed by my *Inner Voice* to these vehicles through a divine turn of events. There was no question that they had my name on them and I was clear about the circumstances that fit their arrival into my life.

The distinction is that most of us are not hearing what is true for us. We are instead focused on the *Outer Appearances* with their bombardment of marketing, advertising, and peer pressure telling us what we need and who we are. And we are hearing these messages consistently throughout each day in all areas of our lives. We are hearing them because we are *Above The Neck* in our *Thinking Mind*.

Your *Thinking Mind* would surely never allow you to drive your mother's twenty-five year old car—you know, the one with the big dent in the center of the trunk from the time she backed into the UPS Truck—to a restaurant with valet parking, and with your friends in the backseat! But once you transition *Below The Neck*, we might be told to surprise our friends and drive to that restaurant in the old rig. Your *Inner Voice* will know if it's for their egos' highest good. Try not to smile *Above The Neck* in that moment!

Look at how we pack our daily schedules at the risk of feeling stressed and overwhelmed. Or how we justify the expense of certain material purchases that we think we need, but then feel pain every month when the bill comes due. Or order extra courses at a restaurant though we aren't even hungry, but everyone else is ordering in a similar manner so we feel obligated or entitled to do the same.

We are overextending ourselves to meet the expectations of others based on the *Outer Appearances*. Many of us spend significant amounts of our hard earned money on things that don't fit our life. We are not hearing the truth of our *Inner Voice*. It is time to change.

Once you connect with your *Inner Voice*, you will live in a *Conscious Awareness* that will help you to create a lifestyle that is more aligned with your truth.

How can I cut my expenses that are no longer a fit?
What can I sell on Craig's List that no longer serves me?
How have my social needs changed?
Do I truly enjoy doing what I'm doing in my free time?

Your world will greatly expand in ways you never saw coming when you drop *Below The Neck* and allow Your *Inner Voice* to guide changes in your life that no longer fit *Who You Are*.

Personal Story
Home Office and I Don't Do Food

At the age of thirty-one, my *Inner Voice* directed me to move from Montana to New York City to pursue a career singing jingles on radio & TV commercials. I had previously owned and managed a successful restaurant for six years, but my *Inner Voice* wouldn't let me sit back on my laurels. I was bored out of my skin.

New York City eats up money, and with the cost of singing coaches and classes, in addition to living expenses, I had to create some type of supplementary income. So I started working as a waiter for catering companies. This gave me a flexible schedule to pursue singing, and it was also a great opportunity to see some of the most incredible private living spaces in this city—and to meet their occupants. As time passed, many of these clients approached me directly to cater their parties. Being *Consciously Aware*, I had to face what was true for me at that point in my life; having owned a restaurant, I knew that I never wanted to manage a commercial kitchen again.

You may wonder, "How can he have a catering business without a kitchen?" Well, I began by making all my decisions from *Below The Neck*. I started a catering business. And I didn't do food!

Acting from my *Inner Voice* guidance about my truth, I could stay *Below The Neck*, *Just—Say—Yes*, and take one step at a time. You will be shown the same in your life choices. Your *Inner Voice* will lead you.

Another truth at that time in my life was that I believed it a wonderful luxury/necessity to earn a living out of my home office. You know the drill, wear the pajamas while you're making money. Just because I grew up in Montana doesn't mean that I don't enjoy looking out at the snow from inside my warm and cozy office!

Today I manage a thriving boutique catering business with the rich and famous of New York City as my clients from that home office in my apartment. All I did was *Just—Say—Yes* to my truth, and then let my *Inner Voice* guide me along that path.

An additional truth is that I work only with clients that I absolutely enjoy. I will not work again with anyone who does not appreciate my staff and our efforts. It's one of the perks of being the boss. My truth comes first. As will yours.

Had I let my *Thinking Mind* have any say about having a catering business without a kitchen, and based out of a home office, it would have said NO you can't do that. My *Inner Voice*, however, knew what was true for me. All I needed to do was honor that inner truth every step of the way as my *Inner Voice* led me forward.

The truth of your* Inner Voice *will change your life, right from the beginning, the first time you act on it.

Chapter 5
The Importance of Your **Inner Voice**

MY *INNER VOICE* IS the most important part of *Who I Am*. I depend on it for every decision I make.

It is my truest compass. It stops me from making decisions based on *Outer Appearances,* which on a daily basis might include the input of others be they family members, friends, or business colleagues.

My *Inner Voice* emboldens me to take the truest and bravest actions of my life—actions that my *Thinking Mind* would never allow me to consider.

My *Inner Voice* is reflected in how I express myself. I am more emotionally available in a conversation. I more clearly set and vocalize my boundaries. I am more at ease with expressing compassion, more comfortable with speaking from insight. I no longer resist expressing love. I give thanks freely, and I feel and express gratitude more deeply than ever before. Voicing these truths keeps me present each day.

There are times when I hear my *Inner Voice* strongly urge me to review situations where I have given away my power or hurt someone by something I've said or done. It pushes me to rectify these situations.

Are you using your *Inner Voice* in your life?

Do you feel your *Inner Voice* pushing you to take action on anything right now?

How aren't you being true to *Who You Are*?

How aren't you letting your *Inner Voice* provide insight to your truth?

Personal Story
The Spanish Villa and the GMC Yukon

One day in late Spring 2001, I sat at the desk in my New York City apartment wrapping up affairs related to my catering business before I left for Spain in just two days' time. I would be visiting a friend, who had several homes around the world, at her villa.

Her *Inner Voice* had prompted her to invite me. Having met each other in a writing class three years earlier, we had become close enough friends for her to initially invite me to Easter dinner at her country house an hour outside of New York City. During dinner she heard herself asking me to come and visit her in Spain. I can still recall how she laughed in surprise at that moment, when this invitation came up from inside her, without any mental thought that she was even planning a trip to Spain. Her husband commented from across the table that he didn't realize that either. My *Inner Voice* would not let me say no.

So there I was several weeks later, my *Thinking Mind* fully engaged in pouring over employee schedules, when up from inside me came the feeling that I was supposed to buy a friend's GMC Yukon that was sitting in Montana. I immediately thought (*Above The Neck*), "What the hell is going on?" I was so startled that I said out loud to the wall in front of me, "I don't need a car and haven't needed one in the fifteen years I've lived in New York City." Then I leaned back in my chair, took my arms off my desk, and stopped everything I was doing in order to listen to my *Inner Voice* as it spoke to me.

I did not negate the importance of this seemingly outlandish thought that came up through me despite being so focused on all my work. My *Thinking Mind* didn't see how I could afford to buy this car, but as I continued to build Self trust as I honored my *Inner Voice's* guidance, I didn't allow my *Thinking Mind* to harp on that thought any further. I chose instead to exercise faith in what it would have me do next now that it had my attention.

I felt directed to call my Montana friend. From what I could remember, she'd mentioned a month earlier that her Yukon was for sale. She buys a new car every few years, and there is always a waiting list of buyers who are eager to own her gently used cars because they are so beautifully maintained. She was a little startled when I immediately asked if she'd sold the Yukon. She said, "It's really strange, but it hasn't sold and this has never happened before."

I told her that I felt like I was being directed to buy it. She was confused, not sure she heard me right because she knew that I did not need a vehicle in New York City. So I said it again. And then she started to laugh in the realization that the car hadn't sold because it had always been mine to buy!

After our phone conversation, I got up from my desk, and paying no heed to the chaotic thoughts in my *Thinking Mind*, walked over to the bank and filled out the paperwork for a car loan. Within two hours I was approved. Before the plane left the runway for Spain I owned a GMC Yukon. And yes, everything else in my office got done as well! It would be a year before I realized that buying this four-wheel drive vehicle was an important step toward a future *Inner Voice*-fueled adventure in Montana!

If I didn't hear my *Inner Voice*, trusting it and acting on its guidance, then I wouldn't find myself receiving and accepting invitations to travel throughout the world or driving the cars that are just waiting for me to accept them.

I trust that my* Inner Voice *will lead me forward each day for the rest of my life and in the direction of my Highest Visions.

Chapter 6
The Freedom of Your Inner Voice

THERE IS SHEER JOY in the freedom you experience as you follow your *Inner Voice's* guidance. It is a freedom that adds dimension and color to your life. Additional depth and meaning to your self-expression. Freedom comes into your life as soon as you begin to hear, trust and act on your *Inner Voice's* guidance.

Take a look at your life. Be honest about where you aren't allowing yourself freedom to live it your way. You may become aware that your needs have changed and no longer fit your lifestyle. New desires may bubble up from within you.

You may be directed to take time to hike on weekends. To accept the dog you've wanted for the past ten years. To become aware that you've felt for some time that you deserve a spa retreat. To know that you will stop using television as your relationship time with your loved one.

We aren't taught to keep freedom at the forefront of our life choices. Instead, our *Thinking Mind* overshadows what we know inside to be true for us.

Can you feel your *Inner Voice* as it pulls you to make changes in your life?

Are you trapped in your daily lifestyle and not honoring the inner knowing that pulls you to make the changes that will bring freedom?

Are you bogged down with debt because you don't hear your

Inner Voice telling you that honoring your personal freedom should be the priority in your actions?

Ask yourself:

Is this more house than you need considering the house payment versus the additional free time and a reduced work schedule that you could enjoy by downsizing?

Is that car payment out of line with the car that meets your needs?

Is this career choice (or move) going to provide the freedom you desire or are you just taking the job because you need to pay the bills?

Can you see how your *Thinking Mind* and *Outer Appearances* got you into situations that do not create freedom?

Shifting *Below The Neck* and into your *Inner Voice* offers you the freedom to be emotionally available in your life and relationships. Now *THAT* is a freedom to experience! What in the heck would a world filled with emotionally available people look like? Wow!

Honoring your *Inner Voice* makes you free to no longer feel the need to meet others' expectations of you. For many people, this freedom alone would transform their lives.

The freedom that your *Inner Voice* offers for self-expression and personal signature is boundless. Think of that joy you have when you come across your favorite color expressed in the exact item for which you're shopping. Or the bliss you experience at the taste of your favorite dessert. Or the satisfaction of a cool glass of ice water that quenches an hour's worth of thirst. This is the boundless energy that awaits you when you choose to hear, trust and act on your *Inner Voice's* guidance.

Do not allow your *Thinking Mind* to persuade you that your *Inner Voice*-directed freedom is mere fantasy. The freedom you have when you live through your *Inner Voice* is *REAL*!

You will always know—no matter how subtle or powerful the feeling—when you are *NOT* honoring your *Inner Voice*:

You're spending time with people with whom you're bored or don't enjoy.

Your day is devoid of quiet time as you run helter-skelter from task to task.

You're comparing your ability to that of someone else.

You're dating someone with whom you feel unfulfilled.

Your *Inner Voice* has most likely been sending you red alerts in these situations, and for quite some time.

When you are connected to your *Inner Voice* and you act on its pull:

You are drawn toward, and bring into your life, those individuals who stimulate your creativity and add value to your life, as you do for them.

You give yourself the gift of quiet time to consider the truth of your *Highest Visions* and open your life wide to more expansive connections and opportunities.

You allow the self-expression that is *You* to come up from inside in all its creative power.

You are single, but remain open to a life partner with whom you are a match, as your new partner will be with you.

Freedom will always result when we live from the inside out. When we begin to express what is true for us. There is no replacement for the feeling that comes from the freedom of expression.

Design the life that feels true for you and stand in the center of that freedom.

Personal Story
Sandals and a Suit

I was once the guest of a friend who lives an internationally mobile lifestyle. One night in Europe as we were heading out for dinner she suggested that in the future I might be more comfortable if I wore sandals with my suits instead of the heavy, hot shoes that I had brought with me on the trip. Now I like to think that I'm teachable, and my intention is to be conscious. So I implemented her suggestion when I returned to New York.

One evening I stopped at a bar after a business meeting. I'd worn a beautiful suit and a new pair of hand-made sandals. As I waited for a friend to meet me, a woman came over and introduced herself. She said that she represented a group of people in another area of the bar. Their attention had been drawn to the juxtaposition of my suit with the sandals, and they found the combination a terrific idea. The group wanted to know what I did for a living because their conservative firm would never allow the guys to wear something this dynamic!

I told her that I owned my company so I didn't have to follow *Someone Else's Rules.*

This episode has repeated itself many times over the years as my freedom to express myself activates people to tell me they can't express themselves in their work place. Hello! What is wrong with this picture? If self-expression is important to you, then where in the heck did you leave your packhorse? Load up and relocate your campsite! While you're receiving your paycheck at your current post, apply to other firms and seek out new work environments where you can express your freedom. Keep the packhorse tied at your desk until you get the call to head'em out!

Within a decade or so of exploring my freedom to wear sandals with a suit, I saw an ad for a company that specifically stated that it allowed employees the freedom to take vacation whenever they wanted—as long as they got their work done. I realized that finally it seemed that 'things they were a changing!'

As You Hear, Trust And Act From Your* Inner Voice's *Guidance, You Will Discover The Freedom To Be Who You Are and To Accomplish What You Came Here To Do.

Chapter 7
The Power of Your Inner Voice

THE POWER OF THAT voice inside you knows no bounds. Most of us have not yet experienced its full potential. Too many of us have no awareness of how this power could be used each day.
So, how in tune are you to act on a hunch, follow up on an insight or take action on a gut feeling? Until you connect with your *Inner Voice,* you're not!

You can't step into your *Inner Voice* power and let it lead you forward until you are aware of it and willing to trust and act on it.

You awoke this morning *KNOWING* you should check on canceling your magazine subscription. When you called, it was the last day of your billing month. Wow! You avoided being charged for another month!

You had an *INSIGHT* to reschedule your haircut appointment without asking yourself why. When you hung up the phone, it immediately rang and your biggest client requested your presence at an urgent last-minute meeting.

You had a *HUNCH* bumping you all morning to check flight prices for an upcoming trip and found they dropped $200 since yesterday. You booked your flight.

Consider water flowing through a garden hose spray nozzle to visualize the power and the unique flow of *Inner Voice* guidance coming up into our *Thinking Mind* each day. Our *Inner Voice* is best suited to tell our *Thinking Mind* to adjust the nozzle to spray an area, point the flow in a certain direction, and choose the volume of flow.

However, many of us erroneously rely on our *Thinking Mind* as it chooses to set its nozzle to spray in too narrow or too wide an area. Or to habitually point our energy flow in areas that do not require our attention (distractions) rather than in those areas that best serve us. Or we allow it to choose too little or too strong a flow volume for the task at hand.

And there are too many people who have a big crimp in their hoses!

Your *Inner Voice* guides you with a three-fold power: to adjust the *Thinking Mind's* nozzle settings throughout the day (its focus), to point the *Thinking Mind* in areas that need our attention (its direction), and to vary the amount of flow coming up into the *Thinking Mind* that is needed to address those areas (its efforts).

Observe those individuals around you who may use this power full volume or just half way. Perhaps they have a kink or two in their hose. You can see it in the stress they carry and in their faces locked in the grimace of survival mode. You can hear it in their angry, dissatisfied, self-absorbed, egotistical *Thinking Mind* conversations.

The level of dissatisfaction in their *Thinking Minds* and the power behind it is directly proportional to their resistance to that *Inner Voice* power that is ready and waiting to come up from inside them. Fighting the flow within each of us is akin to fighting the flow of the universe that surrounds us. And *THAT* is a powerful energy current to oppose!

Why is it that we expend all this energy to fight the flow in ourselves? Fighting what we know to be true, fighting our passions, and fighting what we want in our lives? In all instances the answer is simple:

We are living *Above The Neck* in our *Thinking Mind* and basing our decisions on *Outer Appearances*.

We allow our *Thinking Mind* (ego) to believe that it is stronger, truer or more powerful than our *Inner Voice*. We (our physical selves) are the losers in this battle every time. Witness around you the illness, addiction, and emotional pain; the rampant disease, financial problems, and loneliness that ensue when our *Thinking Mind* resists our unique energy flow.

Helping you to become *Consciously Aware* of your unique and powerful energy flow, and how your *Inner Voice* will help you to harness and apply it, is an important part of why I wrote, *Just Say YES*.

Look around and you'll see people at every turn who allow their inner power to flow up through them. You can see it in how they creatively express themselves in their daily lives. You can see it in their lifestyles. Their inner power is reflected by everything in their life.

Personal Story
Little Caesar

I've worked more than a few jobs that my *Thinking Mind* chose as it overrode my *Inner Voice's* guidance to do otherwise.

It might have been the job title. Or the salary that I thought I needed to pay bills. At times it was peer pressure. In all instances, I was living so far away from *MY* truth and *Who I Am* that I'd rationalize some reason for working in these positions. I was justly rewarded with painful benefits including boredom, frustration and dissatisfaction. My emotional pain from not honoring what I knew inside was true for me caused me excessive physical and emotional wear and tear.

Oh Yes! I'd find some reason to bury my head in the sand or put on that lamp shade to hide from what my inner self knew was not true in each circumstance. I would bind and gag its power until finally it was able to free itself and lead me out of the mess I had made.

Like many of us in our early twenties, I didn't know what career I wanted. My *Thinking Mind* rationalized that perhaps I could make a career out of my riding experience and knowledge of horses. As I write, I can feel my skin beginning to crawl. Boy! Was I in a body bag and ready for the morgue when I chose this first ill-advised career track. Had I just dug a hole and buried myself it would have cut out a lot of pain. Oh, I knew inside that it wasn't something that I wanted to do; but because I was living *Above The Neck*, I couldn't 'think up' anything else to generate income.

I applied for a job riding horses for a horse trainer that I had known since childhood on the show circuit despite having no real interest in working with horses in this way. The trainer was a little man with a big ego, a cruel streak, and a quick temper. I came to refer to him (behind his back, of course) as 'Little Caesar.'

My *Thinking Mind (TM)* ran the show as I ignored the bumping from my *Inner Voice (IV)*. As I considered the job opportunity, the conversation between the two went something like this:

TM: "You must call up all the connections that you have and ask them for references. Tell them to call Little Caesar to recommend you directly for the job."

IV: *"You really don't want this job; but ok, he already knows you and what you can do. Why are you doing all this needless extra work to sell yourself? He's lucky to have you."*

TM: "The pay isn't much, but it will be good experience. Experience that you need."

IV: *"Huh? Come again? Didn't you decide that you were finished with horses other than as a hobby, so what's with this good-experience sales pitch?"*

TM: "Ignore the fact that you hate this job and that Little Caesar's actions demean you. You signed up for this, and you need the money that these long six days a week are bringing in."

IV: *"Good Lord! At this rate, it'll be months before you get back on your real track with all this rationalization you're using to stay in the wrong job for the wrong reasons. How much longer must Little Caesar inflict emotional damage on you?"*

Finally, I began to listen to my *Inner Voice* despite my *Thinking Mind* machinations. One day an urgent family obligation necessitated that I drive 400 miles round trip through the night after work. Little Caesar insisted that I be back at 7 AM the next morning. During the drive, I realized that my *Inner Voice* had had enough. Enough of Little Caesar's demeaning words and corrupt work ethics. Enough of my *Thinking Mind's* excuses to remain in that situation. Enough just to keep me awake to make the round trip safe.

As I pulled into work early the next morning, I could *FEEL* that there had been a changing of the guard within me. Now that my *Inner Voice* was running the show, it tested a few ideas of choice phrasing out loud as I cleaned the first stall. I was surprised at how powerful it sounded, and for the first time since I started that job, I felt elated.

Little Caesar didn't know what hit him when he stuck his head in the barn that morning with his crooked grin asking, without any hint of compassion, if I was tired. My *Inner Voice* instantly brought him to hand telling him to get busy with his own chores because I was finished as of that moment. I felt my legs kick into gear, and I walked out the door. I remember being fully aware that Little Caesar was red faced and hopping mad now that he was dealing with the power of my *Inner Voice*, and I felt safe and protected in that moment. No one can argue with that power when you are speaking from inside, even if they don't like it.

I understand now that little Caesar didn't do anything to me. I was the one that had the crimp in my hose—living in my *Thinking Mind*. I had been less than truthful with myself when I justified taking that job.

Perhaps you should ask yourself right now about your current situation, "What am I thinking?" Or maybe you will recognize your 'been there, done that' moment in a previous career decision. Living from our *Inner Voice*, we need never revisit this level of unconsciousness in future career decisions.

Our* Inner Voice *Will Always Point Us In A Direction That Fully Supports Who We Are And What We Came Here To Do. All We Need Do Is Hear, Trust And Act On Its Wisdom.

Chapter 8
The Strength of Your Inner Voice

USING YOUR *INNER VOICE* is like working out at the gym. The more you use it, the stronger it becomes. The more you use *IT,* the stronger *YOU* become. Both you and the people in your life will become aware of your increased inner strength. It is apparent in how you handle yourself, how you speak, and the way you make choices.

The growing strength of your *Inner Voice* is similar to the imperceptible changes to your muscles each time you lift weights. You may not realize your increased strength day by day until one day you suddenly lift a higher weight. Like the physical changes to your body, your *Inner Voice's* strength is felt and seen over time. You are building it from the inside out.

Your stronger *Inner Voice* may become apparent with a friend's simple question asking, "How did you have the guts to make that (difficult) decision?" Upon reflection, you realize the decision didn't appear daunting because you had grown accustomed to your inner strength. At this point in my life, I make decisions from that place of inner strength. I'm not going on record to say that I have perfect (inner) washboard abs, mind you; but they are strong!

To write this book, I activated myself each day by saying three words:

Just—Say—Yes. Those words were my commitment to get

Below The Neck and connect with my *Inner Voice*. Then I simply sat down at the computer and began to write. *Just—Say—Yes* gave me permission to step into the writing experience each day. Whenever I wanted to resist, I'd say those three words again. *Just—Say—Yes*. Today it will be those three words. Tomorrow it will be those three words. *Just—Say—Yes* is the mantra rooted deep inside me.

That mantra helped me to cross the invisible line of my resistance every time. Those words quieted my *Thinking Mind* and its familiar continuous loop: "You're not a writer; you don't know what you're doing; you're a hit or miss speller; you aren't strong at grammar; you couldn't edit your way out of a revolving door; you don't have enough stories for each Chapter; you can't make it through all the days of isolation or the emotional dredging of your guts; your *Inner Voice* will never give you enough material to fill the chapters; you'll never get an agent; you'll never get published."

All *Thinking Mind* loops wreak havoc. That is why it is so important to *Just—Say—Yes* in those moments and drop *Below The Neck* again. That is where your answers and your peace await you.

Personal Story
The Victory Arch in The No!

I'm fascinated by The Arc de Triomph in Paris. It is an immense 'Victory Arch' commissioned by Napolean to honor his Austerlitz victory, and it has come to represent the celebration of all French victories. It is so large that a biplane once flew through it. Talk about a monument to overcoming the 'NOs!' of adversity!

Some of my biggest life victories have come from the NOs! I have confronted.

At first glance, these NOs! (as in 'No Way Through') appeared impenetrable and overwhelming. NO! I won't survive this. NO! I can't face this. NO! This is too big for me. They seemed to be insurmountable obstacles in my life's path:

I can't make it as a singer in New York. NO!!!!
I have to tell my family and friends that I'm Gay. NO!!!!
I have been diagnosed with cancer. NO!!!!
I am being pulled to write. NO!!!!!!!!

My *Thinking Mind* saw only impenetrable barriers that lacked openings at their centers through which I could reach my YES! But through the years, I have come to trust my *Inner Voice* to lead me forward through each of these false barriers.

Each NO! has had at its center a victory arch through which I trusted myself to walk into the YES! of Who I Am.

Each victory is a testimony to the strength of my *Inner Voice* as I went further *Below The Neck* and farther away from the NOs! in my *Thinking Mind*.

The NO! in my singing career meant facing that it was over. The money supporting my efforts was gone. The years of hard work and diligence felt wasted. I stood in front of what looked to be a solid NO!—the painful question of how I would ever begin to start over.

The NO! in admitting that I am gay also appeared impenetrable. It made Mount Everest look like a pimple! Life as I knew it suddenly disappeared. I didn't want to be different from everyone in my life. I didn't want to go through this experience that was dead center in my life path.

The NO! in my cancer diagnosis was a different NO! than you might imagine. The pain of the NO! wasn't that I might die; rather, it was that I had to make personal changes that I didn't want to make. I had to stop eating everything I liked with refined sugar. NO!!! Stop drinking anything acidic—like my coffee and red wine. NO!!!!!

And the NO! that stood solidly in the way of my writing was the thought of having to get back on the horse. It just seemed too hard, too emotional, and too isolated. NO! Out of the question!

Each of *YOU* has your NOs!

I'm not happy in my marriage.

I'm bankrupt.

I can't express my feelings.

I'm in a career that I hate.

I'm ashamed of where my life is going.

I'm not emotionally available.

I'm scared of intimacy.

I'm flunking out of school and I can't tell my parents.

Why do our perceived barriers activate such strong NOs!?

We don't want to leave the herd mentality and face our unique life path.

We don't want to be shunned or gossiped about for being different.

We don't want to become an entrepreneur to create a life that's true for us.

We don't want to see our personal fears and issues smack in our face.

We don't want to do our individual work.

We don't want to see the end of our life.

We don't want to take responsibility for being *Consciously Aware*.

We don't want to face the fork in the road that we can't see beyond.

From the NO! in our lives, we must pass through the center of our Victory Arch to stand in the YES! on the other side!

Through the NO! in my singing career, I was lucky to work with some of the top singing and performing coaches in the world. I can't imagine my life or me not having experienced living in New York City. It has been one of the most important springboards to who I am today. Yes! Victory!

Through the NO! of facing my being gay, I have passed through the most important Victory Arch of my life walk. Being different has allowed me to develop a level of inner trust that few people experience. This trust has opened up my life. I write with an *Inner Voice* confidence that doesn't need approval. Yes! Victory!

Through the NO! of my cancer diagnosis I see each day as a dance. It's about changes that I need to make *ANYWAY*. It's not about fear. It's not about how long I have to live. It's about facing *ME*. It's about trusting *ME*. The diagnosis isn't about cancer. It's about becoming *Consciously Aware* of what's lying underneath that I need to address. Yes! Victory!

Through the NO! of being called to write, I am living an adventure that I never expected. As I review my writing, my *Thinking Mind* can't believe what I have found inside myself. What if I hadn't passed through my Victory Arch in the 'NO! I don't want to try writing?' I would have missed the YES! of the writer inside of me! Yes! Victory!

In the words of Steve Jobs, "Your time is limited, so don't waste it living someone else's life...Have the courage to follow your heart and intuition. They somehow already know what you truly want to become." *New York Times 2005.*

I encourage you to write down four of your NOs! ... and then walk through the Invisible Arches of each one to the YES! of Who You Are on the other side! Trust your *Inner Voice* to pull you through what only *APPEARS* to be an impenetrable NO! You will find your Victory Arch—your Arc de Triomphe—in the YES! that awaits you on the other side.

Let *Your* Inner Voice *Guide You From The NO! In Your* Thinking Mind *-Through Your Arc de Triomphe—To The YES! That Awaits You On the Other Side.*

Chapter 9
Becoming Aware of Your **Inner Voice**

WE MUST FIRST CHOOSE to become aware of our *Inner Voice* before we begin to effectively utilize its power in our daily life. Believe me it's worth the effort! So whether or not you are fully on board 100%, let's just step into it from wherever you are right now. Hang On... *Just-Say-Yes* and take one step forward, saying the following aloud, "I am now aware that I have an *Inner Voice* that can guide my life." Whew! Congratulations! It's that easy.

You have made your verbal commitment to honor its guidance. Now just go on with your day. Starting today and in the days and weeks to come I want you to write down in a notebook, notepad, or diary *ALL* of the thoughts that come up into your *Thinking Mind*. Yes, each and every one—no matter how 'trivial' you *perceive* that thought to be. The vast majority of these thoughts will be 'To Do' items that require some sort of 'follow through' effort.

It might be a thought out of nowhere to call a friend this afternoon; a thought to pick up more Kleenex when you head out from work at the day's end; to make an appointment for the oil change on your truck; change phone companies to a more economical calling plan; or upgrading your AAA to a Gold membership in case you take an extended road trip. It doesn't matter how small or insignificant the thought is. *WRITE IT DOWN!*

If some of these To Dos can be handled with a phone call right now, I encourage you to do it, or as soon as there is an opening. Attending to these quickly frees you up.

Give no further thought (The 'Hows' and 'Whys') to these To Dos that you write down. Just be aware of them as they flow up into your *Thinking Mind*. Write them down (or quickly handle them) and then let them go.

Each of these written thoughts has a unique energy associated with it. You will come to see the importance of letting that energy be guided by your *Inner Voice* to show you the order that you will address each To Do today or in the days or months to come. Do not allow your *Thinking Mind* to decide which order that it wants to attend to them!

It is easier to become aware of your *Inner Voice* if you start with the everyday errands. The key is to be *Consciously Aware*; in the past you might have just rushed through them and not recognized the value of this process of following an energetic pull. It is important that you learn to *feel* the activation from the flow as your *Inner Voice* starts to lead you.

Whereas in the past, your *Thinking Mind* wanted to control or judge each thought that showed itself, creating a bottleneck that blocked the flow, it will now start to allow these To Dos to pass right through it.

You are now starting to *Just-Say-Yes* to your inner flow.

Your *Thinking Mind* will soon yield to your *Inner Voice*; it will no longer sit like a boulder in the middle of a stream forcing everything to flow around it. No longer will control or judgment stemming from *Thinking Mind* resistance block or impede your decision to take action on those To Dos.

Once you commit to honor the flow of your To Dos, you will become more *Consciously Aware* in your daily actions. You might be driving down the highway and find you're suddenly aware that you like a certain vehicle grill. Or that you are now attracted to a building that you have passed five days a week for two years and never thought about until now. You might suddenly become aware of a feeling to buy flowers for your spouse, a feeling that came up in you out of nowhere, without reason. You could suddenly become aware of thinking of your pet or a friend in the middle of a conference call.

You *DO NOT* need to know what each thought is about in these unexpected moments.

You *DO* need to be aware that these unexpected thoughts *ARE* happening and that they can lead you forward to create a life that fits you. They are pieces of your life-flow's energy that will fit together in time. The process is not about busyness; it is about preparing you to shift.

As you shift into *Conscious Awareness*, soon too will the matters about which you become conscious begin to shift. You may suddenly become aware of a feeling that you need to change your evening schedule without the slightest clue as to why. *NOW* is where you will see the proof in the pudding as you honor the feeling and change your schedule, acting on faith alone and trusting your *Inner Voice*.

Being *Consciously Aware* could bring you together with someone you haven't seen in twenty years that unexpectedly stopped by your house, whom you would have missed had you proceeded with your original schedule. Remain aware of the flow of these feelings (energy connected to a thought) that come up in you to alter your plans, change your direction, or change a prior commitment. The process is preparing you for those life-altering milestones in the future.

Becoming *Consciously Aware* of what you like is an added benefit as you gain experience in connecting comfortably with your *Inner Voice*. You will notice that the things you like have their unique energy in addition to those that you no longer prefer. This will become an important distinction. Especially when you become *Consciously Aware* of the energy you dislike and realize that you have carried it far too long.

Personal Story
The Invisible Line

My deep involvement with horses set the stage for my early recognition of that certain 'something' that was going on inside of me that I would later come to know as my *Inner Voice*.

At fourteen, I was still a beginning horse competitor, though I'd had quite a few lessons. I lacked confidence and was certainly not very self-aware at this stage. I perceived at the time that most of the other kids had 'more'—talent, experience, and fancier horses. I was the average kid who felt overwhelmed by the *Outer Appearances*.

During one horse competition, however, I realized as I exited the ring that I couldn't remember any of it happening. Not one bit of it. Everything seemed to be a blur. It had gone so fast.

Suddenly I heard my name over the loudspeaker. I'd won!

I was confused and shocked. A fellow competitor I barely knew remarked, "It's about time you started winning." I said incredulously, "I can't believe I won." She laughed and replied, "You had a better go than the rest of us and you deserved the win."

I had a better go? I couldn't remember anything about my performance! It was then that I had the feeling I'd crossed an invisible line. Something inside of me had performed the routine. I had not been in my (*Thinking*) mind at all. I was too young and unaware to realize that I'd gone *Below The Neck* and allowed my *Inner Voice* to take over during the performance. At most, I recognized that invisible line. The rest was, well, you know, invisible.

About three years and numerous horse competitions later, I'd made the final cut out of fifty-five competitors and was in the middle of performing my routine. My horse moved at a smooth gallop. I was focused only on staying out of trouble with the other horses and contestants around me.

As I rounded the corner at the end of the arena, suddenly everything stood still, frozen in that moment.

I remember facing the audience in the stands, and I can tell you, thirty years later, the names associated with each friendly face I saw. In that moment up from inside of me came a feeling that I'd won the competition even though I was only halfway through it. The next thing I became aware of was my horse still loping along having made the turn. I was already almost to the other end of the arena.

Later, as I sat in the line-up listening to the placings being announced ... In 6th place ... 5th, 4th, 3rd, 2nd, ... I felt that exhilarating chill come up from inside when I was announced as the winner. While I was still too young to have explained or described the power of my inner awareness in that moment, I got it loud and clear that something inside of me had definitely made itself known!

These are two early examples of feeling a power inside of me before I had a name for it. Before I ever believed it was anything. Before I had an understanding of it. Before I could describe it. And way before I would use its power to guide me. But I felt it, and I never forgot the truth of that feeling.

Only years later would I become familiar with the phrase *"Inner Voice"* as I began to understand its value and importance as a tool to direct my life.

Connecting with *Inner Voice* energy is like learning to ride a bicycle in that moment when you find the connection between your inner and outer balance. You are aware of the shift because you have crossed an invisible line where the within and the without is balanced. No more need for training wheels!

Rather Than Asking "How" Or "Why," Go Below The Neck And Trust Your* Inner Voice*'s Guidance. It Will Always Lead You Forward.

Chapter 10
Hearing your Inner Voice

*I*NNER VOICE IS ENERGY. It is a Feeling. It is a Knowing. It is an Awareness.

The first step into hearing my *Inner Voice* is to honor the feeling that suddenly (or sometimes slowly) comes up through me. I have come to accept this knowing that is ready to show me something; leading me to do something; making me aware in ways I hadn't been a few moments earlier.

There will be times you won't know where that first step is leading you: making a phone call without having a clue as to what the conversation will be about; having a sudden feeling to take the next left turn or to pull over for a few minutes; an urge to take an alternate route for no apparent reason. Try it just for fun. You're not hurting anyone, right? I promise it's not painful!

Hearing your *Inner Voice* as it urges you take these simple steps will prepare you for those future life-altering moments when you are fully *Consciously Aware* and act in ways that will bring you closer to *Who You Are*.

It could start with you suddenly feeling directed to call three people to come for dinner and you don't have any thoughts of why you called them or what you'll be serving them. It could well be that they are not supposed to be available to accept your offer because it is not about dinner. Your *Inner Voice* could be directing you to connect with each of them for a specific reason that will be revealed to you in those conversations. You simply need to *Just-Say-Yes* and proceed with each call.

When taking your first steps, it is not about putting yourself at risk. In fact, the only risk that your *Inner Voice* will ever offer is that you will break through to *Who You Are* and *What You Came Here To Do*. It will never place you or others in harm's way.

Rather, these simple exercises in hearing your *Inner Voice* are about spreading your wings to act in ways that feel right to you as you honor the *Feelings Connected To Thoughts* about which you are becoming *Consciously Aware*. They come from a place of inner love and trust. You'll know them when you feel them.

Consider the exercise of buying a gift for a loved one to gain practice in hearing your *Inner Voice*. It can be glaringly uncomfortable for some of us to face how unattached we are in the process of our gift buying. So step into your commitment to become *Consciously Aware* of your feelings as you make your way through a gift purchase. Your awareness is heightened through the process of following and honoring *Inner Voice* energy. You need not have any *Thinking Mind* tension because a gift can easily be exchanged!

Your daily wardrobe decisions are another simple exercise to become *Consciously Aware* of and honor your *Inner Voice's* direction. I only wear clothes that reflect the energy of the inner me. I now honor this direction on a daily basis.

One of the more exhilarating exercises to practice hearing your *Inner Voice* is to take a road trip scheduled only through your inner guidance: when to drive, where to stay, or route changes. Stop to spend time along the way only as you feel directed. Your inner guidance may influence the course of your trip for a variety of divine reasons: joy, protection, least stress, or scheduling. You will experience everything that is divinely intentioned once you learn to get out of your *Thinking Mind* and go *Below The Neck*. That is where you will begin to hear your *Inner Voice*.

Have fun! Knock yourself (from the inside) out!

Personal Story
The First Time I Heard My Inner Voice

Becoming aware of my *Inner Voice* for the first time was a

serious shock to my system. A shock that I hope to alleviate in you by writing *Just Say YES*.

It began as I walked down the sidewalk at 9:48 AM on my way to class on the second day of winter quarter, my sophomore year in college, when I suddenly experienced an *OVERWHELMING* emotional feeling that literally exploded from inside of me. It was immediately followed by a thought that caught me completely by surprise. My *Thinking Mind* was stunned.

The burst of energy connected to this feeling/thought told me to quit my classes and simply ski for the rest of the college quarter! I stopped dead in my tracks. I was confused and shaken, now aware of this powerful inner feeling that wasn't there moments before. What in the hell just happened inside of me? Five steps earlier I had been fine! I had never felt anything this emotionally overwhelming ever before!

Quit my classes? Ski for the rest of the quarter? My dad will kick my ass!

I was being pushed to reject everything my parents, upbringing and schooling had taught me about following the rules. In these moments, I didn't know that this turn of events was my *Inner Voice* speaking to me. It was just this 'thing' that happened inside of me that I couldn't deny. Couldn't explain. And yet somehow I knew that it was real.

I sat down on a bench trying to figure out what had just happened. I next became aware of trying to understand why no one had ever mentioned this powerful voice that was inside of me.

Why wasn't I given any tools to prepare for this moment?

Why was there no previous guidance from my parents or from my schoolteachers to prepare me for the day that this voice inside would make itself known to me? No one had ever sat me down and told me *THIS* fact of life!

My *Thinking Mind* yelled at full volume, "No! Don't do it! This feeling inside you isn't real! Why would you do something that no one around you would conceive of doing? What will your dad think?" While my *Thinking Mind* continued to tell me that this inner feeling couldn't be real, the powerful voice inside of me did not rest. It kept pushing me with a thought/feeling to chuck my father's money that I'd just used to pay for the semester two days earlier.

Here I was in a situation that I could not explain, justify, or dare seek advice. Yet in this moment, I knew whatever was happening inside of me was pivotal; my father's needs were instantly no longer first in priority. His feelings were no longer more important than what I felt inside.

It was simply about me somehow having the guts and the strength to listen to and trust the inner me.

Then a feeling came up in me that the money wasn't being thrown away. Rather, it was paving the way for an experience that the inner me knew was part of my true learning. It would be a lesson that would influence all of my future decisions.

So I did it! I quit all my classes and didn't tell my father. Despite the deep fear of where my actions might lead, something inside pulled me forward to ski every day. It was my first true leap of faith.

It was only years later that I came to see how this moment was connected to the center thread of my life path. Though I didn't know it that day, part of the center thread of that *Just-Say-Yes* moment was tied to my writing this book. It was my first significant step into *Who I Am*; a conscious decision to let the energy/knowing to act on a *Feeling Connected To A Thought* lead the way. It was in a direction away from the *Outer Appearances* and rationale of my *Thinking Mind*.

Your Choice To Hear Your* Inner Voice*'s Guidance May Be The Fork In The Road Moment That Will Lead You To Discover Who you Are And What You Came Here To Do.

Chapter 11
Trusting your Inner Voice

TRUSTING YOUR *INNER VOICE* is a continual building process, brick by brick, moment to moment, that eventually creates a solid foundation and structure on which you can rely. It serves as a powerful catalyst to activate your *Conscious Awareness*. Trust is both an important factor in and a result of acting on your *Inner Voice's* guidance. It is a vital key that will help to open the doors to *Who You Are* and *What You Came Here To Do*.

Trust is *NOT* outside of you. Rather, it begins deep within you and is developed through practice. Have no worries if you currently feel unable to trust either yourself or others. This is simply your *Thinking Mind* second-guessing your *Inner* Voice. Once you learn to trust your *Inner Voice*, you need never wonder about trusting anyone else but *YOU!*

Trust-based (*Inner Voice*) decisions are lessons that free us to move forward, at ease with our past actions. They don't carry self-doubt, even if they don't work out in the way we expected in our *Thinking Mind*. I know that I live from a place of trust within and from my *Inner Voice* because I take full ownership and responsibility for past decisions that I made that (seemingly) did not work out as I anticipated they would. *Inner Voice* Trust is an energetic cord tied to powerful dreams rooted deep within us. It allows us to know that our dreams are real.

Any lack of connection to our dreams and trust in our *Inner*

Voice is apparent when we find ourselves looking across the fence at our friend's perceived easier path or greener pastures. Standing in the trust of my *Inner Voice*, I know I will manifest what is true for me in my backyard. It is never about what lies across the fence. Rather, it's always about staying *Below The Neck* and out of my *Thinking Mind*.

There is a vast difference in "Where's mine?" triggered by *Thinking Mind* lack and "It has my name on it" triggered by trusting *Inner Voice* guidance.

When you become *Consciously Aware* of a *Feeling Connected To A Thought* that is true for you, in that moment you must trust yourself, owning that it is real and true enough for you to act.

For example, if you are directed from inside to purchase a special item, you must trust that *Feeling Connected To A Thought* and act upon it, knowing that you will be shown every step of the way forward. Through each step, the actions you take bring you to even deeper levels of trust. If you are directed from inside to purchase a home or a car or a new outfit, and you act on it in 'faith,' then from that moment you have stepped into trusting yourself.

You are trusting that you will be shown every step of the way forward—that the money is there to purchase the house; that the car is divinely right for you; that there is an occasion tied to the outfit or you would not have felt the direction to purchase it.

Actions based on *Inner Voice* trust bring us closer to living our lives from the place of *Who We Are*.

Personal Story
A Leap of Faith

The dark bank of clouds seemed to suddenly materialize as I rushed along the creek looking for a crossing. As the rain started I knew my time was up. I had two choices: trust my fancy three year old colt, Classy Cadet, to make a jump that most horses couldn't or wouldn't attempt, or backtrack forty-five minutes through soil that would quickly turn into bog holes I couldn't see. The possibility of him pulling a tendon forced me through my mental fear to an inner decision.

At sixteen I wasn't aware of the term *Inner Voice*, but

something inside of me in that moment, and despite my fear, trusted that he could make this jump. And I knew if I didn't get to my trailer soon, I would never be able to drive out through the three miles of muddy road.

As I showed him the edge of the bank he snorted and jumped sideways. He'd been raised in these hills and was familiar with the terrain. I'd been riding Cadet for the past six months. He was more horsepower than anything I had ever owned or ridden. He was smart and athletic, but the quality that made him special was his willingness to try anything that was asked of him. More than one person told me, the day I got him, that I had bought the horse of a lifetime.

I found a spot with a slight downhill slope that aided my take off and had flat ground directly across on the other bank. Showing him the edge a second time, he snorted and tried to dance sideways, but I held him until he stood still.

Trotting away, and deciding on the distance for my final approach, I hoped he'd gotten the idea of what I was going to ask him to do. I was in turmoil about the best speed going into the bank. Should I come in at a fast trot to make sure he'd have his feet in good position for take off? Or come in at a gallop for added momentum?

I held his head tight with one rein in each hand to keep him moving straight for the bank's edge. As we came forward at a strong trot I increased our speed the closer we got to the edge. I still remember feeling the knot in my stomach as I drove him forward with my legs.

I was caught off guard as he suddenly leapt into the air and his neck hit me in the face, blinding me with pain. My shirt hooked on the saddle horn and stopped me from falling off as his back feet left the ground. My only memory during the jump is of pain and trying to hang on. My ribcage came down on the saddle horn from the impact of his front feet landing on the far bank. My shirt tore as I was thrown back into the seat of my saddle as one hind foot struck solid ground. Then my saddle dropped down as his other foot slipped back over the edge of the bank. He groaned and strained forward, somehow pulling us onto the bank.

As I slid down from the saddle, holding my ribs and trying to get my breath back, I knew I had to keep him walking in a circle.

Blinking through the tears of the pain in my forehead and nose, I tried to see if he was limping as the rain began to fall harder. Suddenly he stopped, shook his whole body, and started bobbing his head in reaction to the rain. It was as if to say, "Get me in that trailer and let's get out of here." I stiffly climbed back on and we headed for the truck, and soon made our way home.

Years later, when Cadet and I were ranked nationally as one of the ten best teams in working cattle, I finally understood the distance his willingness had carried me on that jump. Many times since his passing, I would have given anything for his partnership on my own life jumps. Yes, he was the horse of a lifetime.

I trusted my *Inner Voice* that day way before I knew what it was or had a name for it. I share this story to remind each of us that we always have the inner push before we're aware of its powerful guidance in our lives.

NOW Is The Time To Trust Your* Inner Voice. *You Need Never Second-Guess Yourself Again.

Chapter 12
Acting on Your Inner Voice

YOUR LIFE WILL TAKE on an entirely new dimension when you begin to act on your *Inner Voice's* guidance.

In the past, we have all stopped short when we followed a hunch only so far, or acknowledged but then ignored a gut feeling. Or when we only talked about an insight without acting on it. Don't blame yourself. So many of us have lacked role models that would have helped inspire us to act on our *Inner Voice's* guidance. No one ever taught us about its powerful place in our lives, or that it even existed. But now through the pages of *Just Say YES* you can learn to hear, trust and act on it.

I can imagine your *Thinking Mind* saying right now, "What if I try(-ied) it and didn't work out!"

Ex—Cuse—Me? Look Around You and See How Much Hasn't Worked Out In Your Life While You Have Ignored Your Inner Voice!

Stepping into action seems like a major leap, but *Just–Say–Yes* and take one step forward at a time. It won't be long before acting from your inner wisdom adds an exciting element to your life. It is a whole new dimension to living. It involves an unknown part of me that has come to feel so very right.

Acting on my *Inner Voice* is an important part of each day. It has come to feel natural, as it will for you. It has proven itself in many ways, and I have grown to trust it implicitly. People in your life will begin to notice changes in you and the actions you take. They may be affected directly or through their observations of your process. Either way your actions will catch their attention because you are acting from the truest part of yourself.

Have fun with this process and do not be concerned with the effects your transformation has on your peers. You are now their teacher. They have their process too and in many cases you will be activating them to step into their truth. Their *Inner Voice* might activate them to move forward with you or take them on a path of their own even if it's out of your life.

It is also important to understand that when you hear, trust and act on your *Inner Voice's* guidance, you are directly connected to your *Highest Visions*.

That's right. You are no longer separated from those dreams and desires that retreated deep inside you when you trusted and acted from the realm of limitation in your *Thinking Mind* when it told you that they were not possible. Don't worry they're still alive and well, and with your *Thinking Mind* out of the way, you will feel more powerfully connected to them than ever before.

Personal Story
Run and Turn In A Way That Is Natural

In my early years working with and competing on horses, I became aware that a vital training component was to let them *Run And Turn In A Way That Is Natural* for them. I offered direction and guidance, but I had to first become *Consciously Aware* of the natural way that the horse chose to act on what I asked it to do. Each horse was different and I would listen for my inner guidance—that feeling that would come up from within me—to determine the best course to work together.

My *Inner Voice* likewise pulls me forward to *Run And Turn In A Way That Is Natural* for *ME* each time I act on its guidance despite my *Thinking Mind* being surprised at times by the blind curves that appear on my path. These *Twisty Turny Parts* can seem intimidating and overwhelming despite the trust I have in my *Inner Voice's* guidance.

Just recently, my *Inner Voice* pushed me to mail a deposit for a puppy that has not yet been born... and I live in a NYC building that doesn't allow dogs! Talk about a *Twisty Turny Part!* What was my *Inner Voice* up to?

Over the past ten years my *Inner Voice* had occasionally revealed to me that I'd be joined onstage by a miniature Australian Shepherd as part of the talks and workshops associated with *Just Say YES.* Four months before I completed the book, my *Inner Voice* pulled me to begin searching Australian Shepherd websites all over the country to educate myself. But I never knew why or when the puppy might appear, much less how I would have it given my lifestyle. My *Thinking Mind* told me that I wasn't ready yet.

But once I mailed the nonrefundable deposit, I became *Consciously Aware* that what had to shift to bring the puppy into my reality was *ME*! Since my building doesn't accept dogs, I would be leaving my NYC apartment after 25+ years. What?!!

In these moments when my *Thinking Mind* races with all of its limiting thoughts based on the *Outer Appearances*—Where will I go? Why give up a rent-free lifestyle? How am I going to care for a puppy with my schedule?—I simply stay *Below The Neck,* trusting that my *Inner Voice* will pull me forward through the *Twisty Turny Parts.* I also remain *Consciously Aware* of signs that validate my trust.

Within several months I received that validation. Within minutes of finalizing the cover layout for *Just Say YES,* I was notified that *MY* puppy, Razzle Dazzle ("Raz"), had been born! I guess since they'll be sharing the stage spotlight, they decided to arrive on the scene together!

The act of sending the puppy deposit fully committed me to take *Just Say YES* out into the world. I was no longer able to cling to my apartment, neighborhood or lifestyle. My *Inner Voice* showed me that I was ready to move forward, regardless of what my *Thinking Mind* told me. Don't ever expect your *Inner Voice* to allow you to run and turn in a way that is *familiar*!

And the *Twisty Turny Part* continues. As I prepare to publish, *Just Say YES,* my *Inner Voice* has guided me to look into winter cottage rentals near the Connecticut shore. Acting further on its guidance, I have also purchased a ticket to fly from New York to

Tucson, pick up Raz, and then fly back into Hartford, Connecticut rather than NYC. But I have yet to find the Connecticut property that feels right to me, much less signed a lease! But I will continue to trust my *Inner Voice,* knowing that the cottage will appear in perfect timing and location, and with the perfect lease terms.

(Update: Within three weeks of purchasing my ticket, I signed an eight-month lease on the perfect cottage and with the perfect terms. My Inner Voice *guided me to bid on this property that my Thinking Mind told me was out of my price range, and my bid and terms were accepted! Thank you* Inner Voice *for leading me through the Twisty Turny Parts to the perfect house!)*

Your Inner Voice *Will Pull You To Run And Turn In A Way That Is Natural For YOU. It Will Pull You Through The Twisty Turny Parts As It Guides You Forward On Your Unique Path.*

Chapter 13
Living With and From Your Inner Voice

IT IS SAID THAT early tribesman had a connection to the earth and their surroundings that was based in other than the spoken word. Rather, they knew that they would be shown where the animals and food that they needed to survive were located. This unspoken connection has been described as an 'ancient wisdom' that guided them. This wisdom was their *Inner Voice*. The same wisdom upon which you are now drawing that is at the root of your being. Each of us is ready to reconnect with this wisdom so that we can live with and from this part of our deeper self.

Living with and from your *Inner Voice* will guide you to make daily decisions that fit the present moment. You will find purity in your process, trusting that you will receive a direction from within to find your way forward, no matter the chaos of a present situation. You will become your own person, relying solely upon your inner dialog for the answers you seek. You need no longer look outside of yourself for the answers.

As children, our innocence is strongly rooted in this wisdom. We are born into an immediate connection to the inner self that the vast majority of us unfortunately lose as we grow into adulthood. As kids we acted out scenarios from within without being conscious of what was going on around us; we seemed to live in different worlds and dimensions right next to our parents on a Sunday afternoon in the living room. Maybe it was jumping around fighting an imaginary dragon. Perhaps it was belting out tunes in some fantasy world. Regardless, we were connected to our inner source and lived exclusively in freedom and creativity.

A friend recently told me that she was driving with her 5-year-old daughter and out of the blue the little girl said, "Mommy do you know that dying can be a really good thing?" My friend found out later that day that her father had passed suddenly from a massive stroke four states away about the same time her daughter made this statement. I see this as the little girl's connection to her grandfather and as an energetic connection to the ancient wisdom that ties us together.

Imagine the child you have seen in its stroller, actively focused on some inner self that has it singing or having a conversation in an imaginary place. This is the place inside of the adult 'us' that we rediscover as we tap into our *Inner Voice*. Now don't try to use the excuse that you can't access this place because you won't fit into your old stroller. Remember that you have upgraded to a car that is as fine a place as any to have a conversation with yourself!

With or without the stroller, doing the work might just connect you with your life partner, or that car you keep feeling, or a winning lottery number. It might put you on the right road at the right time to place someone in front of you so that you can help change a flat tire or call a tow truck for your favorite movie star. All the while and no matter the circumstance, you will be interacting with them from your *Inner Voice* in a connected way with inner wisdom, compassion and true intention. By the way, the latter example is one I shared with a famous movie star that was all *Inner Voice*-directed. Out of that chance meeting came a connection with a well-known movie producer who became one of my best catering clients.

To *Just—Say—Yes* offers you the opportunity to revisit your truest self and rebuild the connection to your inner and ancient wisdom. Especially in today's world, that connection is a strong anchor helping you to stay present and live a grounded and more balanced life despite the daily chaos that you otherwise face. You just go with it and live in the inner flow with the attitude best summarized by the phrase, "What you think of me is none of *MY* business!"

Are you seeing and connecting to the ancient wisdom that is in your children? That is in your parents? In the people you care about? The ancient wisdom to which you were fully connected as a child will add depth and insight to your life and to the relationships with those you love.

Personal Story
Medicine Doll

It was in my uncle's country grocery store near his rural Montana farm that I saw a black doll in its box sitting high above me on a shelf when I was five or so years of age.

I still recall some fifty plus years later my immediate connection with the doll in that moment. I can feel the well-worn old hardwood floorboards beneath my feet as I stood there staring up at her. Something deep inside of me was tied to something greater than the physical doll.

Let me be clear. It wasn't long before everyone in the store knew that I was not leaving without that doll. Already a divine force at that tender age, I was ready to do battle with anyone who thought otherwise. What in the heck a black doll was doing on the shelf of a rural Montana country store in the 1950s was proof positive that higher forces were at work that day.

The doll brought me closer to my grandmother than I ever would have grown because I insisted that she make clothes for it. In this moment I can still draw up around me like a blanket the warmth of absolute love that I felt spending time with her as she sewed the doll's wardrobe. I realized years later that I would have had no other reason to spend time with her in any other way without this doll linking us together.

It's an energetic connection that I can still feel as I picture her sitting in her favorite sewing room chair. I can hear her laughter as she accepted specific instructions to execute my design vision. I was aware even then that she appreciated who I was as she helped me to accomplish my dream. We each enjoyed the connection of experiencing our life forces and our ancient wisdom working together.

I took 'Blackie' (my not very original doll's name) to my first day of school, much to my parents chagrin. My mother tried in vain to talk me out of it, but I would have none of that. When I got home my mother wanted to know how my day had been. I'm not sure if I told her that the kids teased me, but she said that I told her that I decided not to take Blackie the next day.

And we wonder why we lose our innocence and our early connection to see the things we can no longer see as adults. Our inner light dims, weakens or disconnects as we get older and move farther away from the connection to our wisdom connected to our *Inner Voice* as our innocence gets banged and dented.

Though Blackie remained at home, her power and importance in my life remained significant. I should have called her Medicine Doll such was her influence on me and on my parents, who shifted into the unconditionally loving and understanding adults that they became in this lifetime. Blackie served as the vessel that helped to activate the ancient wisdom within my folks that they would need as they raised me. Blackie's presence in my life at that time forced them to kick into gear much earlier than perhaps they had planned. I know that my dragging that black doll around rural Montana was definitely an experience that my parents never saw coming.

You see my parents had adopted my two siblings and me from different birth families when we were each under a year. Witness the ancient wisdom and the connection to spirit that brought each of us into my parents' home by divine plan. As soon as we were old enough to understand, they told us that we were special and that they prayed for years for us. Through the years, I must confess there may have been more than a few days that I tested their faith and the veracity of their adopting me.

Within a year or so of Blackie's appearance in our lives, I remember my father asking me never to lie to him. He told me, "I am willing to grow through anything with you." He proved that to me year after year. I can still feel the ancient wisdom emanating from inside of him as he uttered that unconditionally loving statement that day. Both he and mom were rare parents. I had more than a few friends wanting to trade in theirs for mine.

Their love and support was rooted in their inner wisdom. It just came out of them. My father especially lived from his *Inner Voice*, although he would never have called it that or even had a thought about how he connected to it. To him it was just a natural way of being. Oh sure, he went *Above The Neck* on occasion, like the time he realized that I'd spent half his silver dollar collection on candy, but it was rare for him to remain in his *Thinking Mind* for long.

His memory serves as a reminder to me that we can connect to our inner ancient wisdom at any time. It's always ready and available. We don't even have to remember it. It can be activated by something every day in our life. We need only hear it when it speaks.

An Inner Wisdom Rests Within You. It Is Always Ready And Available. You Need Not Remember It. Something Every Day In Your Life Will Activate It.

Chapter 14
The Clarity of Your **Inner Voice**

A<small>T</small> TIMES THAT 'VOICELESS voice' sounds so clear that I want to look to the person next to me and say, "Pardon my *Inner Voice* if it disturbed you." It's that loud and clear! Or that *Feeling With Words Around It* may be so strong that it catches my attention like police lights flashing without the siren sound. I just can't deny its powerful clarity when it has my attention.

It might be several words that come up through me, "Don't buy the green coffee mug," as I pass a store shelf or "Sign up for a *Time* magazine subscription," as I stand at a magazine rack. I could be walking through the park and hear the words, "Call so and so now! DON'T WAIT until you get home!" I never know when it will come, and I have learned to act on it as though time is of the essence. *DON'T PUT IT OFF! DON'T SECOND GUESS IT!*

There is a clear distinction between acting on the pull from *Below The Neck* and acting on a thought impulse coming from *Above The Neck* in the form of *The I Needs* and *Connecting The Dots*:

The I Needs. As in 'I need a house with a bigger deck for that one time a year that I have people over to watch the 4th of July parade' or 'I need to buy that horse trailer because it's a great price, in great shape and I would love to have a horse.'

The *I Needs* many times have an outlandish justification accompanying them.

Connecting The Dots. As in IF I get a cheap flight to Rome, and AND get a cheap hotel AND find a friend to go with me to split the costs, AND I get time off from work, AND I earn/save the money for the fare, THEN I can go to Rome.

Connecting The Dots is trying to think up each step instead of hearing/feeling your *Inner Voice* directing you in the actions to take. Our *Thinking Mind* is very adept at plotting and planning—*Connecting The Dots*.

When you find yourself in that place, remember to go *Below The Neck*. There you will find the clarity of your inner pull as it guides you forward.

With clarity comes a raised *Conscious Awareness*. It's a new way of living that activates and expands your life. It will become very clear when your *Inner Voice* is trying to show you something. As you raise your *Conscious Awareness* of the experience that results from acting on your *Inner Voice*, you will see the benefits of these unexpected levels of clarity and how they can greatly aid your daily life.

Taking action on the clarity coming from within, you will replace the old *Thinking Mind* thoughts that had you *Connecting The Dots*. The inner you in whom your trust will grow exponentially will begin to regularly out vote your *Thinking Mind* in your daily decision process. This level of inner clarity lets your decision be finished—really finished—once it has been made. Talk about the freedom to act!

Remember that an important part of this process is that you are continuing to raise your awareness and gain trust in yourself. The material results are not the only objective; awareness is also a benefit and a powerful step forward on your path. Down the road, the clarity of an action that you took several days, weeks or years earlier will be more clearly revealed to you. For now, it is important to welcome *Conscious Awareness* as part of your clarity as you grow forward in your life.

Personal Story
Throwing Out My Television

Working on a writing assignment at my desk one evening, I struggled with my desire to also watch the Summer Olympics.

They had always been a big deal in our household. When I was in high school, my father and I planned all our farm work around that telecast.

The TV in my New York office was the last of three sets I'd previously owned. It sat on a high shelf attached on the wall behind me. Every time I went to look at the screen, I had to turn all the way around from where I was writing at my desk.

I heard my *Inner Voice* loud and clear when it told me that I could not write and watch TV at the same time. My *Thinking Mind* immediately justified that, NO this was the Summer Olympics and they wouldn't happen for another four years. In the moment, I allowed my *Thinking Mind* to override my *Inner Voice's* direction.

I began to write and swivel, write and swivel. Then the TV needed some adjustments. So I got up on my stepstool and started working on it. This up and down process went on for twenty minutes. Now I wasn't getting *ANY* writing done or enjoying the telecast!

And then somehow as I stepped down from the ladder after yet another adjustment, I hooked my foot in the cord and pulled the TV crashing to the floor. The case broke but the tube kept playing—and *STILL* needed adjusting. Which now was *REALLY* annoying!

In that next moment, I gained clarity and became *Consciously Aware* of the message from my *Inner Voice*; if I wanted to write not just my assignment, but more importantly, the book that I felt coming up from inside of me, then it was time to let go of TV. It was time for me to be an active participant in *MY* dream instead of an observer of someone else's dream. I got it! To the trash went the set. It was the last one I have ever owned.

Pushed from inside that day, I shifted to make my writing a priority over watching TV. I shifted deeper into *Conscious Awareness* that there was a book bumping around in me. My *Thinking Mind* did not know what the book was about or how all *THAT* was going to happen. However, I trusted that the process would reveal itself as the energy from inside pulled me forward one day at a time towards what I felt was true.

Your Inner Voice Will Always Make Itself Heard When It Really Counts. Beware The Consequences When You Try To Ignore It

Chapter 15
A Personal Journey with Your Inner Voice

LIVING FROM THE INSIDE out is about our personal journey as we honor the pull of our *Inner Voice*. It is no longer about the Monday through Friday work routine. There is freshness to each day that replaces the staleness that otherwise sets in when our *Thinking Mind* runs the show. Our inner wisdom encourages us to stretch ourselves in different and unexpected ways in both work and play.

Change is a constant in life whether we like it or not. As we come to accept this universal law, we honor the awareness that we have an *Inner Voice* to guide us toward greater freedom. As we become more *Consciously Aware,* we awaken to a whole new world in front of us.

We can let go of the greatest lies that our *Thinking Mind* tells us: That security exists outside of ourselves. That security is achieved by maintaining the status quo. Rather, the truth is that we have free rein in all areas of our lives when we start working from the inside out. Our *Inner Voice* is all the security we need to embrace the universal Law Of Change.

So let's agree to stop resisting everything that our *Thinking Mind* tells us we aren't ready to embrace or can't understand or can't afford.

Say out loud,

"I commit to stop living a life led by resistance in every

decision, opportunity or daily task! I embrace my new life led by my Inner Voice that I trust completely, and in which I will find all the security I need to manifest all that is true for me in this new awareness!"

Welcome to the new life flow in your personal journey! You have made the commitment to quit leading with resistance. So now things will start to happen. For some wonderful divine reason the inner you will start to feel the energy of 'The Sky Is The Limit!' Your personal journey will have begun, led by your *Inner Voice*. This may be the biggest *Fork In The Road* decision of your life to date! *CONGRATULATIONS!* You have *Just-Said-Yes* from the inside out.

Once I actively embraced my *Inner Voice*, one of the first major shifts I noticed was truly becoming a 'People Person,' a concept that up until that moment I had never considered. I was guided to all kinds of people that I would otherwise never have met or considered spending time. My life opened up exponentially because of it.

I have also become *Consciously Aware* that my *Inner Voice* is guiding me toward the people with whom I am now ready to interact and toward the situations that are specific to my life path. I'm always moved when I reflect on the experiences in which my *Inner Voice* placed me well before I became *Consciously Aware* that I was activated to participate in them.

Within this life flow I have found the power and joy of my personal journey.

Personal Story
Luncheon with Dr. Mannion

During one of my *Above The Neck* moments, I decided to transfer schools and major in pre-med, in large part because there was money to be made in it. I enrolled in a private Catholic College because it was noted for the having a high percentage of graduates placed in Medical School. I was an older student and non-Catholic when I transferred in.

As head of the department, Dr. Mannion was intimidating both in manner and position to almost everyone in school. He expected students to be focused and committed. He was serious and stern when he spoke, and his piercing eyes kept you in their grip until he was done with you. It was his belief that you were there to study, and he made that clear from day one. Everyone was tense whenever they had to go to his office and discuss something. The collective fear that came up when he asked a question in class was palpable.

I sat in the front of his class where I felt pulled to be by my *Inner Voice*. Believe me when I say that it wasn't so that I could answer questions like all of the eager smart kids sitting around me. Curiously, about a month into the class I realized that I was not afraid of Dr. Mannion. After several months, I visited his office to ask him about the results of a test. During our brief exchange, I suddenly felt my *Inner Voice* push me to ask him out to lunch.

My *Thinking Mind* snapped to full alert as it heard the invitation pass over my lips. I remember the knot in my stomach and feeling lightheaded as the oxygen supply was cut off to my brain. My *Thinking Mind* yelled that this was a terrible idea!

As I stood in front of his desk, my *Thinking Mind* perceived that Dr. Mannion was trying to make sure that he had heard me clearly in preparation to bite my head off. But as he sat staring at me, I began to notice the curl of a smile forming on his lips as he said, "No one has ever had the guts to ask me to lunch. They are all too afraid of me. Yes, I'd like to go to lunch with you, Erec." My *Thinking Mind* silently reflected, "Thank You Jesus!"

And so it was that Dr. Mannion and I began having lunch every month. We talked and laughed about many things. Just as I mentioned in an earlier Personal Story that acting from your *Inner Voice* will catch the attention of people in your life, word spread like brushfire that Erec Lindberg and Dr. Mannion were lunching with each other. What did it all mean? By then I wasn't concerned about these *Outer Appearances* because during those lunches my *Inner Voice* did most of the talking. It asked him all the questions I had inside, the ones that I would never have had the opportunity to ask in an office or classroom setting. Out of these questions came an inner clarity for my life path.

During our third lunch, I became aware that I was finished with the pre-med program and instead I wanted to own a restaurant. Dr. Mannion was supportive and fully respected my decision. Through our time together I'd come to better understand that something inside me was pulling me in another direction that my *Thinking Mind* had never considered.

My *Inner Voice* deserves full credit for this opportunity to expand. My *Thinking Mind* was a chicken sh-t and would *NEVER* have allowed me this sharp turn in the road. My lunches with Dr. Mannion were key to my receiving the information that I needed to take the next turn in the road and buy a business instead of going on in pre-med classes. Thank God for my *Inner Voice* coming up through me with that luncheon invitation, even if it did shake the structure of my physical and mental being.

As You Step Into Your Personal Journey And Trust Your Inner Guidance, You Will Experience A Clearer Vision As You Proceed Forward. The People And Places Will Be Supplied.

Chapter 16
Growing into The Energy of Your Inner Voice

As YOU RAISE YOUR awareness by hearing, trusting and acting on your *Inner Voice*, you will feel the energy flow up from inside as it continues to grow more powerful. What begins as a mere pulse will grow into a strong, steady push from inside. This is where the fun REALLY begins! The increased energy flow will help you to expand into areas of yourself that you have not used and about which you may be as yet unaware.

The growth in your *Inner Voice* flow is two-fold: you step into your Self, and you step into your Life.

All of a sudden it feels like you can experience life as you have always wanted. Current opportunities expand and new opportunities present themselves in proportion to the increased energy coming through you.

You *Inner Voice* will activate new areas of energy flow as it pushes you to face your truths. These flows could include expansion in your career *OR* the realization that it is no longer fulfilling. This additional energy might also reactivate the nine-year-old painter in you. It might push you to write, take singing lessons, rent a cabin for the summer, join a seaside timeshare, enroll in Toastmasters, or ask your divorced neighbor out on a date.

You may never have considered these scenarios, but the energy coming up from your *Inner Voice* is now making you aware of a strong pull to dive into them. Let's remember that the stretch is about expanding beyond the things with which we are familiar and comfortable. It is about (re)discovering those parts of you that have remained hidden or buried perhaps for years.

Avoid the pitfall of going *Above The Neck* into your *Thinking Mind* to analyze why you suddenly want to take a yoga class, write a blog, or work in an upscale jewelry store as a second job on Saturdays. Maybe you have always been a gemologist inside, but you haven't been aware of this until your *Inner Voice* energy activates you.

Take a moment to consider whether your current life is filled with distractions? Or how you feel on Sunday evening when you realize that Monday morning is around the corner? Are you happy? Growing into your *Inner Voice* and honoring your awareness to step into its pull will reveal more of your Self than you ever expected.

Inner Voice-directed growth is never about *preparing* for what you are being pulled to experience. You'll just feel the inner energy leading you into the unknown experience. *Just-Say–Yes* and take the next step. It's about time you let it come out! Let it flow from inside and up through you, and experience its truth about *Who You Are*.

Personal Story
The Restaurant

As I grew more comfortable living from my *Inner Voice* after hearing it at the age of nineteen, I still wasn't aware enough to understand the difference between a *Thinking Mind* 'thought' and an *Inner Voice Feeling Connected To A Thought*. Consequently, I made a bunch of right and left turns on my path forward.

Growing into my *Inner Voice* energy was two-fold: it took me to the next step into my *SELF*, and it took me into the next step in my *LIFE*. Growth is found in both our personal unfolding and in our life experiences.

When I left the pre-med program at the Catholic school, I was certain that I wanted to open a restaurant. I could feel the pull of a business coming up from within me as more of the entrepreneur in me started to surface.

Unbeknownst to me, my *Thinking Mind* was still very much a part of the decision-making process, although I was not yet *Consciously Aware* enough to realize it. It held the belief that I could live happily ever after by owning a Mexican restaurant in a beautiful mountain town, tied to the pulse of the local university, and with a ski hill close enough that I could work thru lunch and ski every afternoon. Sounds pretty good on paper to the *Thinking Mind*, right?

After six years of owning that restaurant and experiencing that lifestyle, I had received plenty of growth both in *SELF* and in *LIFE*, only my *SELF* was completely bored and consequently unhappy with the *LIFE* that it had created.

The entrepreneur in me had succeeded, but it had also saddled me with payroll, seven-day workweeks, and a kitchen that I manned when an employee didn't show up. I learned that owning a business took its pound of flesh even while it was lucrative, and in spite of being a lot of fun at times.

Why did I ever let myself think that making tacos for the rest of my life was the pinnacle of *Who I Am* or *What I Came Here To Do?* My Word! That's scary as I look back now!

My *Thinking Mind* had settled for security and lifestyle over progressive inner growth and truthful living. Sure, there was a picturesque mountain town with lots of distractions and the added security of being my own boss. Yet, I wasn't facing the fact that I worked more long days than I wanted to admit. More importantly, I was sacrificing my inner expansion and creative expression.

My *Inner Voice*, in fact, pushed so strongly against this lifestyle that I felt at times like I was dying inside.

Outside of working, I pursued drinking and other distractions to avoid the truth; I was very unhappy, and I could feel my *Inner Voice* pulling me to New York City.

Our Thinking Mind *Will NEVER Create The Life We Truly Want.*

Chapter 17
Your Inner Voice *and the Fork in The Road*

THERE IS A FREEDOM when you live in the flow of your *Inner Voice*. It is the foundation on which you can rely as you face the daily challenges and life decisions that require you to choose a fork in the road on the way to becoming *Who You Are*.

With every *Inner Voice*-directed choice you make, you gain the strength to face the future forks in your life path with enthusiasm and confidence, instead of the angst and worry that are both part of the process and the result of making a decision from the *Thinking Mind*. Be aware also that choosing the path to *Who You Are* may often lead you away from everything that up to that point looked and felt familiar to you.

In the past when you lived in your *Thinking Mind*, you may have missed these forks completely. Or the forks may have brought such fear of the unknown that you could only choose the path that felt familiar to your *Thinking Mind,* rather than the path to *Who You Are*. Working from your *Inner Voice*, however, you can better understand, accept, and face life changes or obstacles, because your *Inner Voice* is connected to passions and attractions that come from that fork. The *Outer Appearances*, meaning the outsized consequences that your *Thinking Mind* would otherwise create, simply fall away.

Decisions, that in the past your *Thinking Mind* told you had to be made from your comfort zone, will now be made from the freedom of true expression powered by your *Inner Voice*, whose guidance will move you forward without allowing the *Outer Appearances* to exert any power over your choice.

You have already faced a fork in your road as you read these pages having now said Yes! to your *Inner Voice*. Pat yourself on the back. You have chosen the path toward finding your true Self. Hooray for you!

One of the most powerful results of using your *Inner Voice* to make decisions when you face the fork in the road is that you will begin to feel the need to let go of things that no longer serve or fulfill you. You will consciously embrace this shift in activities, people, and possessions that will come into your life or drop away.

Personal Story
A Fork in My Career Path

Once I came to the deeper realization that I felt empty and hollow despite the lifestyle that my restaurant brought me, my *Thinking Mind* finally gave way and allowed my *Inner Voice* to kick into action. Holding myself accountable to *Inner Voice* direction meant staying *Below The Neck* and out of the strong current of the *Outer Appearances* as I faced my reality; My *Inner Voice* was pulling me towards New York City and a career singing jingles for TV and radio commercials. Talk about a fork in the road!

It directed me to list the restaurant for sale. Four interested buyers immediately approached me. I had six years remaining on the lease, but every buyer wanted an additional four years added to it to create a ten-year lease (which was a standard practice in the area). The lawyer who represented the landlord came back with the news that the landlord wanted an additional and ludicrous $30,000 I rent per year to extend the lease. The buyers disappeared.

The landlord's lawyer apparently liked me because shortly after he delivered the bad news, he openly pondered, "I don't know what my client's thinking because you could easily file bankruptcy and break the lease."

My *Thinking Mind* went into spasms. What? Bankruptcy? After running a successful restaurant for the past six years? My *Thinking Mind* told me I would need all the money from the sale to support my lifestyle when I move to New York City!

My *Inner Voice,* meanwhile, told me to talk to my Dad, who as the financial backer would be left holding the majority of the bag. My *Thinking Mind* screamed, "Oh No! Not a good idea. He will be furious!" As I drove the 180 miles to my parents' home, my *Thinking Mind* kicked into overdrive as it considered every possible scenario to justify my actions.

Arriving home, I finally got *Below My Neck* and my *Inner Voice* presented my position to my dad: "I feel pulled to sell the restaurant and move to New York City; the interested buyers have disappeared due to the landlord's demands to change the lease; the lawyer says I could file bankruptcy and break the lease; since you put up cash and stocks to finance my restaurant, you will lose your money."

While yelling was never a common occurrence in our household, the ensuing heated exchange between us was definitely a new fork in *THAT* road! As my *Inner Voice* continued to stand its ground with my dad, my mother watched wide-eyed and silent as the drama unfolded before her.

Yet it was all over in less than ten minutes. My dad paused, momentarily collecting his thoughts, and then said to me, "I don't like losing money, but I don't want you to stay in something that you don't want to do. I want to watch you live your life. Consider this money to be part of your inheritance. We can sell the land and use our assets in the areas that you kids are interested in expressing yourselves."

As he spoke those words, I could hear my dad's *Inner Voice* and feel the power emanating from within him. In this moment, his unconditional love for me reinforced the lesson that following my *Inner Voice* was the ONLY way I would ever live my life from this moment forward.

***Life Renews Itself At Each Fork In The Road When We Act From Our* Inner Voice.**

Chapter 18
Your **Inner Voice** *and The Trailblazer in You*

LIVING FROM YOUR *INNER Voice* will soon turn you into a trailblazer with a new zest for life!

Taking that fork in the road leads you boldly into the unknown, leaving behind a path fraught with boredom, unconsciousness and unfulfilling mediocrity. As a trailblazer, you sit in the pilot's seat checking out the runway as you take off toward an open horizon! You will recognize your flight path by the energetic inner pull that leads you forward.

As a trailblazer, you may not know what to do next or in which direction to head; but you won't have to know the answer ahead of time. Because you are living from the inner knowing that guides you every step of the way, you will feel the answer lying in you, and trust the trailblazer in you (your *Inner Voice)* to pull you forward. No longer will you feel the need to (or will you attempt to) control the unknowns through your *Thinking Mind.*

I want to encourage the trailblazer in you to trust yourself with daily decisions in ways that you never have.

No one has power over the trailblazer in you because the trailblazer is *YOU* activated from inside. As a trailblazer, you no longer need someone to save you, pay your way, or help you survive. You don't need the approval of others, nor do you need to look outside of yourself for someone to give you the answers. Or give you the money you think you need. Or give you the love that you seek. The answers are no longer outside of you.

Trailblazers are teachers whose lives reflect their message. They live as examples to friends, family, and coworkers who see them living in ways that they are too afraid to attempt. They will wonder how you can do it, and they may wonder how you have suddenly had these ideas and had the confidence to act on them.

Trailblazers are inventors and entrepreneurs. Working from their *Inner Voices* as they faced the unknowns in their lives, it was the trailblazers before us that created conveniences that we have in our lives today. Like them, all you need to do is simply activate your bravery software by trusting in your inner knowing. Recognize that it is not about the *Outer Appearances*—not about HOW to do it. Rather, it's about being aware that the answer has always been lying right there inside of you all of the time.

Trailblazers are explorers who choose not to simply follow the rules created by man. Rather they are attuned to and follow the rules of earth and nature as they break the trail for the rest to follow. Consider that it may just be *YOUR* time to lead others forward as you share with them the gifts that you came in to this lifetime to share. Gifts that reflect *Who You Are* and *What You Came Here To Do*!

Personal Story
Roping Lessons

The trailblazer in me awakened that morning on the sidewalk when I heard my *Inner Voice* for the first time. I ditched my class and headed back to my dorm to flop down on my bed and reflect on the morning's events. My *Thinking Mind* was scared, numb, and resistant now that I'd connected to this new power I found within me.

My *Inner Voice* illuminated the truth of what I was feeling inside; that this decision to stop attending my classes and ski was a critical juncture in my life. It wasn't about trying to understand why no one else around me was on this path. I lay on my bed most of the day, rising long enough to eat a quick lunch and dinner. Finally, I went to sleep.

I awoke the next morning and headed for breakfast, not having a clue as to what my actions would be that day. After breakfast, I walked back to my room and felt the pull from inside to start putting on my ski clothes. My *Thinking Mind* immediately started screaming, "No don't do it! You are really going to get it from your father!" Yet I dressed, grabbed my skis, and headed to my car.

As I drove off campus, I was acutely aware that all the traffic was coming towards me as students arrived for morning classes. I was the only one who was going the other direction as I headed towards the ski hill.

For the entire school quarter, I became the trailblazer on my dorm floor. I was well liked, but my chosen path of skiing everyday and all day long activated the students who lived on my floor. (Just as you will activate the people in your life as you allow your inner trailblazer to come forth.) My peers would be feeling the pressure of an upcoming test or a late assignment and here I'd come worn-out physically from a hard day of skiing moguls. Believe me it was confusing for all of us as we walked our individual paths that quarter.

A second powerful experience that quarter affirmed that I must continue to do what felt right to me. Once a week, I would give a roping lesson (I'd been schooled by a world champion) to another ranch kid on my floor. He was always so serious and rigid about following the rules, and he constantly worried about his studies.

It was only at these weekly roping sessions where I saw him laugh and be playful. It appeared he was living his passion during our nickel betting competitions. The following summer he was cleaning a gun, and it somehow went off and killed him. This sad event made me grateful that I'd offered an opportunity for him to laugh and enjoy a different aspect of his college experience.

His short life added clarity that I must trust myself from inside in my life decisions. It made me even more thankful that I'd honored my *Inner Voice's* direction. Spending that winter alone, pushed from inside to ski the slopes, changed the course of my life. It continues to influence how I make a choice or decision today. My *Inner Voice* opened the door for me to become *Who I Am* in this lifetime. The trailblazer inside has led me all these years to write *Just Say YES*.

We Open Inner And Outer Doors When We Honor The Trailblazer In Ourselves.

Chapter 19
Your Inner Voice *and Your* Highest Visions

OUR *HIGHEST* VISIONS ARE those dreams and desires that originate from our *Inner Voice* and are the truest parts of *Who We Are.* Our dreams and desires are those visions that we can feel and see in our mind's eye. They just feel 'right' to us. There have been times on my life's path where my *Highest Visions* have not been at the forefront of my focused efforts. Rather, my efforts were goal-directed, and I have come to see that these goals originated from my *Thinking Mind* as I attempted to *Connect The Dots* toward their achievement.

Dreams and desires that lay deeper within me would pop up at times out of nowhere, but my *Thinking Mind* would discount them as unbelievable and too amazing to be real. Or it would immediately go to the "How Tos" or "How Coulds" and then drop my dreams and desires from my awareness.

At present, however, with my *Thinking Mind* detours behind me, I find that my *Highest Visions* remain safely anchored. They merely awaited my rediscovery of them once I let go of the consequences of my *Thinking Mind's* 'failures' (unrealized expectations) that had overpowered and pushed down these dreams and desires.

Once I whole*heart*edly heard, trusted, and acted on my *Inner Voice's* guidance, I better understood the distinction that my goals were 'thought up,' whereas my *Highest Visions* were 'felt' within me. The latter carry a definitive energy that I instinctively 'know' *IF* I stay *Below The Neck* and allow my *Inner Voice* to lead the way.

For example, much of my early writing experience was too emotionally overwhelming for my *Thinking Mind* to consider that writing a book was a 'real' possibility that emanated from a *Highest Vision* within me. In paralyzing fear, I would approach writing from *Above The Neck* and my *Thinking Mind*, thereby lowering the frequency of my *Highest Vision* down to that of a mere 'goal.' A goal that was accompanied by *Thinking Mind* doubts that I could ever write a book. I was stuck in my role as a 'doer/thinker.'

Goals have a lower vibrational energy because they originate from a *Thinking Mind* that has been conditioned to believe that we must sweat and sacrifice to achieve them. Mere goals don't allow our inner pull to carry us forward easily. The inner pull becomes too big for the *Thinking Mind* to process without becoming overwhelmed. And so the *Thinking Mind* lowers the frequency of the energy in order to accept it at a level that it can comfortably process based upon its belief system conditioning.

So even as the energy of my *Highest Vision* pulled me forward to write a book, my *Thinking Mind* created doubt energy that conflicted with that inner pull, thereby dragging it down. I was left to roll around in confusion that came hand in hand with thinking. That is until I chose to completely drop *Below The Neck* where I could fully hear, trust, and act on my *Inner Voice* to honor that *Highest Vision* to write *Just Say YES.*

Further examples that distinguish my *Highest Visions* (those that feel vast and whose energetic pull direct me to create a fulfilling life) from mere *Thinking Mind* goals include:

Owning the feeling that *Just Say YES* is not only real, but published and a best seller in the US, Canada, and globally. My intention is to shift global consciousness forward.

Connecting to my inner knowing and using those spiritual tools that resonate with me to create freedom in whatever areas (including personal expression) in which I feel pulled to create.

Creating a world talk that will crack people open to see *Who They Are* and *What They Came Here To Do*.

Opening my heart enough so that I am the first one to reach out my hand to greet in equal measure a friend or (perceived) enemy.

Demonstrating to the world that it need not be true (nor ever has been) that the older we get, the more we let our *Highest Visions* slip away.

All of us have at some time ignored our *Inner Voice* as it spoke to us from the place where our *Highest Visions* live. Instead we remained in our *Thinking Mind* where doubt lives, and where we either shut out or down-graded our *Highest Visions* to mere goals, adding the sweat and sacrifice and suffering that we (falsely) believed was necessary to achieve them.

Personal Story
Asking My Dad If He'd Do It Differently

Much of my life has been spent in the pursuit of my *Highest Visions* and being led by my *Inner Voice*. However, it was not until I fully understood that I must remain *Below The Neck* and out of my *Thinking Mind* that I began to appreciate the ease of accomplishing those visions without the worry or doubt that ensued when I tried to *Connect The Dots*.

I was lucky that my adoptive parents, and especially my Dad, allowed me the opportunity to always keep a toe-hold on my soul's *Highest Visions*, one of them being to bring a message about our *Inner Voice* to the world, in part, by writing and publishing *Just Say YES*.

While out hauling hay one day with my Dad, my *Inner Voice* suddenly asked him, "Would you do anything in your life differently if given the chance?" He was surprisingly silent, which was unusual since he was smart, insightful, and always verbally available. His response was further delayed as we headed back out to the field for another load of hay.

I always marveled at how my father's life fit him like a kid glove. He seemed to have his own pace with work and play, a steady rhythm by which he lived. He always had time to stop back by the house for a midmorning coffee or a couple hands of cards with friends who may have come by. He seemed to stay out of distraction, enjoy the process of his life, and still get everything handled with ease.

For years, my *Thinking Mind* pondered whether I could find a career that fit me with the same joy and freedom that he shared with farming. Notice that part of my process was using my *Thinking Mind* to observe my father and try to *Connect The Dots*, while my *Inner Voice* was feeling the truth in the way he lived his everyday life.

As we returned from the field and began unloading the truck, he finally responded to my earlier question by saying that his initial response would be that he should have taken the bigger farm that his dad had wanted him to have.

Mom and he met and married in California during the war. When it was over, they returned to Montana where he already owned land. When his dad offered to help him buy a larger place, he and mom talked it over and decided they didn't want all the responsibility that came with it. My grandfather's ranch required a number of full-time hired men, and Dad knew deep within himself that he did not want the daily burden of directing workers.

Still in his life review process, he told me that my question caused him to reflect on that earlier decision to turn down the offer of a larger farm and the additional income it would have provided. While he had always supported every one of our interests, considering that I was the most 'expensive' of the three children triggered him to suddenly question if he should have done his life differently for all of us.

And then he looked me in the eye and said, "I wouldn't do my life any differently."

In that moment, I knew inside that I, too, wanted to speak that truth at the end of my life.

Back then I was not aware enough to understand that my father was deeply rooted in his *Inner Voice*, that place deep inside from which he made all of his decisions. Nevertheless, I could feel in how he spoke and lived day-to-day that it was the place from which I also wanted to live my life.

Living mostly *Above The Neck* in my *Thinking Mind* in my youth and early adulthood, however, I set my goals and tried to *Connect The Dots* in an effort to duplicate what I could *feel* he had in his life, rather than allowing my *Inner Voice* to guide me toward my *Highest Visions*.

Writing *Just Say YES* and reflecting on the freedom that I have had to experience every Personal Story is proof to me that I can reach the end of my life and say with heartfelt joy, "I wouldn't do it differently."

***Remain Aware Of The Vastness That You Feel In Your Highest Visions.** This Is Where Your Truth Lives And Awaits You To Step Forward Into It.*

Chapter 20
Raising Your Frequency through Your **Inner Voice**

I WANT TO TAKE a moment to salute you for your efforts thus far as you learn to connect with your *Inner Voice*. Consider this next Chapter to be an energetic marker in your progress. The content we are exploring that includes the Law of Manifestation will further impact *All* of your future decisions in profound ways:

As You Learn To Recognize And Hold The Higher Energetic Frequency Tied To Your Highest Visions, Becoming Consciously Aware As You Connect To And Act On Your Inner Voice's Direction, You Will Manifest Those Highest Visions Into Reality.

Your *Highest Visions* are your deepest desires and dreams tied directly to *Who You Are* and *What You Came Here To Do*.

In order to dial up your frequency to that same frequency of your *Highest Visions*, you must remain *Consciously Aware* to hear, trust, and act on your *Inner Voice's* guidance. This simple truth begins *Below The Neck!*

Consider the concept of your energetic frequency in terms of how you set the dial to tune into your favorite radio stations. Each station broadcasts on a unique frequency. Changing the radio station changes the frequency to which you are 'tuned in.'

Just As You Choose The Frequencies Of Your Favorite Radio Stations, Your Inner Voice Chooses The Frequencies Matching Those Of Your Highest Visions.

As you hear, trust, and act on your *Inner Voice's* direction, you become more *Consciously Aware* of everything that surrounds you. Maintaining that state of being, in turn, raises your frequency. Raising your frequency helps you to better feel your way forward through a heightened perception of all areas in your daily life.

Soon you will attract new people and experiences into your life. At the same time, you will let go of activities, job or career interests, friends, and behaviors that no longer serve you. In time these choices will be replaced by other choices that fit better with your higher frequency.

As I elevate and maintain a higher frequency on a daily basis, I bring positive and lasting change to all aspects of my life. More opportunities to enjoy quality free time, to create emotionally supportive friendships, to enjoy a broader range of stimulating conversation, to experience daily laughter, and most importantly, to validate that I have manifested my dreams into reality.

Even my living space becomes charged with this elevated frequency. For a period of time, my Montana home became a gathering place, an energetic salon if you will. It was clear that those people who walked in the door were directly tied to the frequency I was holding at that moment in time.

Raising my frequency has brought me a significant increase in clarity; those areas that I need to let go from my life that are not a fit energetically become readily apparent. Like a domino effect, as I release my attachment to frequencies tied to choices that do not reflect my *Highest Visions*, other frequencies tied to new interests and ways of expression show up to replace them. These choices will lead me closer to *Who I Am* and *What I Came Here To Do*.

Shifting to a higher frequency has influenced how I earn my income in relation to the effort that I put into earning it. I work less, but earn more. My abundance has been consistently supplied in much easier and more straightforward ways. The key, I have found, is to maintain that connection between elevated frequency and my *Inner Voice*-directed actions through complete trust in what I am directed to do moment to moment.

So what do I mean about elevated frequency in relation to you? Let's use an example of a dream or desire that you may have, such as a trip to Rome, Italy. This dream trip holds an energetic frequency for you. It's an exciting international adventure and the trip of a lifetime. If it's a new car that you desire, so be it. But know that this dream has a different frequency than the Rome trip.

All aspects of your life—things, choices, decisions, and actions—have a unique frequency attached to them. Consider the frequency that is held in the chore of mowing that huge backyard, in one hundred degree heat, on your only day off in the last three weeks. It has a lower frequency than the higher frequencies of a trip to Rome or a new car that are more directly tied to your dreams and desires.

Consider that your highest frequency is directly related to your highest passion in that particular moment. The chore holds a lower frequency than the dream or desire of a trip to Rome. The longer that you can hold onto that feeling of passion or bliss tied to your dream or desire, the longer you remain at that higher frequency. In order to hold several higher frequencies in place, you must prioritize (and in some cases let go of) your focus in other areas tied to lower frequencies.

Your *Inner Voice* serves you well as your guide. In fact, it is the *ONLY* way that you will be able to hold those higher frequencies that match the frequencies of your dreams and desires. It is often the case that your *Inner Voice* will prioritize the frequencies of things, choices, decisions, and actions in ways that your *Thinking Mind* could never conceive of doing moment to moment.

If you rely only on your *Thinking Mind* to prioritize your actions tied to achieving your dreams and desires, you will never achieve or maintain those matching frequencies. Going *Above The Neck* simply disconnects you from, or significantly reduces the level of, those higher frequencies because you are inundated by distractions related to *Outer Appearances*.

None of us were taught at home or in school that in order to manifest our dreams and desires, we'd have to match and hold the frequencies tied to them by remaining *Consciously Aware* of their direct connection to our *Inner Voice*. The *Inner Voice* is the only tool we have that is powerful enough to hold those higher frequencies once we are aware of their truth.

Consistently acting at lower level frequencies (those of distractions and chores), rather than holding the frequencies of our dreams and desires in highest priority, is why many of us are so good at maintaining the former and not achieving the latter. It just seems easier to remain in the lower frequency levels no matter how difficult the realities of those circumstances may be.

It is why we are working in jobs or pursuing careers that don't fit, remaining in stale relationships, and living paycheck to paycheck instead of creating new careers and relationships that reflect abundance tied to the higher frequencies that are a truer fit for us.

When we have an insight that feels true like a trip to Rome, a new car, or writing a book, we must be *Consciously Aware* of the specific frequency that connects to and matches each of these dreams or desires. This is where our *Inner Voice* is invaluable. One of its specialties is to feel an awareness of, and connection to, the specific frequencies tied to our dreams and desires. In each moment, it will lead us to our choices, decisions, and actions that are directly tied to reaching these *Highest Visions*.

All you need to do is maintain a *Conscious Awareness* of when, where, and how your *Inner Voice* is directing you to act and follow its lead. It is an opportunity that unfortunately most of us don't take, and instead we remain *Above The Neck* to think when, where, or how. This latter path will never work out for us.

Be aware of the frequency of something you want to create, something that is true for you. What is the essence of it? Meaning what higher frequency does it represent to you—freedom, joy, excitement, stability, expansion, or self-expression? Visualize and feel yourself aligning with the frequency of your dream or desire *AND* with your *Inner Voice*.

Remember that *YOU* must be a match in frequency with those of your dreams and desires in order to manifest those dreams and desires into reality.

Personal Story
The Frequency of Being Cool

One evening as I sat with friends eating dinner in my Montana home, one of my guests turned to me and said, "You were probably always cool. Some people are just born that way." My initial response, to be funny, was to turn around and look behind me to see if he was talking to someone else. He could have no concept of how far from *THAT* truth my earlier years had been, especially when I had lived *Above The Neck* in my *Thinking Mind*!

I was surprised at his implication that I had somehow always been 'cool.' This was a man whose property might be described as a compound, with a main house, attached guest wing, and horse facility sitting on five hundred acres of forested land in the mountains near my home. He owned several other homes around the country. He managed a hedge fund and seemed to have plenty of financial abundance in his life process. By material standards, he would have to be considered way cooler than me!

I realized that his statement was a reflection of his *Thinking Mind's* need to label its perception of my higher frequency as we interacted through dinner. As I had become more *Consciously Aware*, thereby raising my frequency, I had become accustomed to the manner in which others, like him, perceived me. (You can expect comments about how healthy, young, vibrant, and calm you seem to those around you. And well, yes, cool. You will find complete strangers drawn to you who 'want what you're having,' energetically speaking.)

During the range of our dinner conversation, I related to my guest that I was flying once a month from New York into Montana to host a friend who performed energetic healings on people in a studio I created in a barn down the hill from my house. I told him how amazing it was to have a waiting list of people wanting sessions on a windy, remote hillside in the middle of nowhere. Who knew!

Upon hearing this, he immediately responded, "I want to do that! I want one of those sessions." His wife, sitting next to him, snapped her head around in utter disbelief and exclaimed, "You've never even had a massage!" He retorted, "I don't care, I want one!" She then quickly followed up with, "Well, if you're having one, then I am too!"

As I watched their exchange, another friend in my line of vision at the other end of the table, held her hand up to get my attention and mouthed silently, "Me TOO!!!"

The Frequency of Who You Are Radiates Out From You And Activates Everyone and Everything Around You.

Chapter 21
Your Inner Voice *and* Reading Higher Frequency Material

READING INSIGHTFUL MATERIAL THAT further motivates you to live and act from your *Inner Voice* is one of the best ways to becoming *Consciously Aware* once you start working from inside yourself. The material further elevates your frequency as your *Inner Voice* pulls you forward toward your *Highest Visions*.

I encourage you to ask friends and bookstores for recommendations. I keep a stack of reading material within reach of my office chair. My daily early morning quiet time is spent reading several pages in a book to which my *Inner Voice* has pulled me. You will be amazed at how fast the material activates you to drop into your inner self. Over several weeks, you will find that this practice will elevate your personal and professional insights.

By reading material, I mean the material that resonates best with you right in that moment where you are on your path. For some this may mean material that builds upon deeply engrained religious beliefs. Others may be so turned off by negative religious conditioning that any mention of God or spirituality immediately causes paralysis in their *Thinking Minds*.

Accordingly, it may be motivational or self-help material whose religious neutrality best serves your needs. Remember that this is your life, and you are free to choose your reading material, spiritual beliefs and the tools for reaching deeper into the core of *Who You Are*. You are no longer living by *Someone Else's Rules*.

Choose material that activates and expands you forward, rather than choosing the same type of material that merely reinforces concepts with which you already feel comfortable. You will feel and hear your *Inner Voice* awaken and begin to speak to you. It will have an opinion, inspiration, activation, insight, or pull forward.

In the beginning, some of the books that you choose, or that are referred to you, may not make any sense to you. It's ok to put them aside for now and move on to something that stimulates your *Inner Voice*. There is no coincidence that reading material that expands your awareness will show up in your daily routine. It is part of the process. *Just—Say—Yes*, stay *Below The Neck*, and you will be pulled to the more advanced material in divine timing.

All reading material has a unique energetic frequency that is tied to the material's message. As we connect with and absorb the material's message, we raise our frequency to match that frequency. As our frequency is elevated, we are drawn to a wider range of material that serves to further elevate our frequency and bring us deeper into *Conscious Awareness*.

In most of my reading material, I highlight those passages to which I most deeply pulled. Highlighting holds me accountable to the fact that I actually connected with the frequency of the material's message. It also facilitates revisiting those passages to energetically reactivate myself to those frequencies.

Revisiting the highlighted passages to which I feel pulled further enables me to observe which material has brought teachings/beliefs/awareness that have demonstratively produced results in my life. In turn, those teachings/beliefs/awareness become the tools that I incorporate into my daily practice to maintain and expand my life *Below The Neck*.

I purchase most of the books that are recommended by friends, and I do not allow my *Thinking Mind* any leeway to edit the reading material that is drawn to me. Rather, I simply log into Amazon or head to the nearest bookstore and order it. At times, I have waited up to six months or a year before I actually read certain books I previously purchased.

Or, I may start a book immediately only to put it down as I am drawn to read other material. In all instances, I am opening and expanding my awareness. Time passes and I connect with the material that I couldn't absorb several months earlier. Material that seemed impenetrable for weeks or months is now easily digested, and I wonder what stopped me previously from reading it? Sometimes it seems like I am reading a foreign language; other times the author's voice doesn't pull me in until I am ready to hear the message.

I have come to see in these instances that the material reflects a higher frequency than I am used to at the time. It might be that my belief system was too rigid for me to expand and absorb the material. In all cases, I have ceased to question 'Why' many years ago. Instead I have come to accept that it is simply divine timing when my frequency is elevated in that "Ah Hah" moment to match that of the material.

I also have periods where I have four or five books in process at one time. In the quiet of early morning, I alternate among the different frequencies contained in the books' messages. I feel alive and insightful as the reading material triggers energetic expansion and brings a truer awareness to me, guided at all times by my *Inner Voice*. Most joyous are the moments when the material opens me up to a whole new way of looking at my experience. This is when a new pathway is activated within my consciousness and I feel so much growth.

Oft times I order material for friends that are not ready for its higher frequency, but my *Inner Voice* pushes me to do it, knowing that there will be a future frequency connection for them. It may be much later when I receive a call that they have just read the book with ease. I never question my inner guidance and its connection to their inner guidance because I have come to see that they will become more *Consciously Aware* in divine time.

Personal Story
Bejeweled Digits

Raising my frequency through reading higher vibrational material, I have likewise raised the frequencies of my life experiences. Trusting my *Inner Voice's* guidance, I act within these frequencies despite the *Twisty Turny Parts* that my *Thinking*

Mind can't begin to comprehend.

As a direct result of having raised my frequency in this way over the years, I have also attracted interesting and creative people into my life. One such couple has invited me several times to the Caribbean island of St. John to share a vacation house.

I had always wanted to visit this area, and on my first trip I flew in to St. Thomas two days early to read, relax, and look around. Once my friends arrived, I would meet them to take the ferry over to St. John.

Walking down the hill from my hotel for dinner that first night, I crossed a random street that was lined with jewelry stores as far as the eye could see. My *Thinking Mind* momentarily sneered in judgment of the volume of horse-trading that most likely occurred along that tourist trap.

Yet two days later as I left a restaurant intending to soon meet my friends at the ferry, up from inside of me came a thought/feeling from my *Inner Voice* that I was to buy an emerald ring! That day! Immediately!

My *Thinking Mind* registered surprise and immediate resistance to the thought/feeling. It reasoned that over the past five years, I had felt the energy of an emerald ring several times. I had even once inquired about its cost at a NYC jewelry store. But in this moment my *Thinking Mind* insisted that I had only fifty-five minutes to head back to my hotel, check out, and wheel my bags down to the ferry. By all *Outer Appearances,* this idea was ludicrous!

My *Inner Voice* simply laughed and said, "Easy Peasy!" And with that I rounded a corner to find myself on the street lined with jewelry stores that I had sneered at two nights earlier!

I felt tension in my body as I began to act on my *Inner Voice's* direction and peer into store windows in search of a ring. All the while, my *Thinking Mind* continued to warn me that I had no idea how to even choose a "good" emerald!

My *Inner Voice* responded that I knew two things. Firstly, that I could trust it to lead me in choosing *MY* ring. Secondly, that I would spend around $1000.

While I mused that Elizabeth Taylor wouldn't have shopped for a gem at this price range, my *Inner Voice* reminded me that this process of purchasing and wearing the ring was really about elevating my frequency and being even more *Consciously Aware*. It felt right that I would wear on my finger the energetic frequency that an emerald carries.

At the third store I entered, I felt drawn to an emerald ring with a price tag of $1800. "Way out of *YOUR* budget," my *Thinking Mind* told me. And yet I followed my *Inner Voice's* guidance as it twice directed me to begin walking out of the store during negotiations. Within ten minutes, I was out the door with *MY* emerald ring. The final cost of my bling? $1050! Thank You, Thank You, *Inner Voice*!

As I made my way to the hotel and then on to the ferry with time to spare, my *Thinking Mind* remained shocked at what had transpired. Towards the end of my island adventure, it eventually came to accept my purchase, reasoning that this was an isolated incident driven by the joy of visiting a place about which I'd always dreamed and doing so with great friends.

"Not so fast on the limiting thoughts," my *Inner Voice* chided me several days after I returned to New York. "You have nine other fingers. Time to visit the Manhattan Jewelry Exchange!" What?!!

My *Thinking Mind* was apoplectic that I could even consider such an investment. Who could I trust to make such purchases amidst the immense warren of dealers in the Exchange district? How could I afford such extravagances? Who was I, a spiritual Liberace?

And yet I knew that my *Inner Voice* was pulling me into even higher frequencies that the additional stones on my fingers would bring. In fact, over the next nine weeks, I purchased nine additional rings from jewelers to whom my *Inner Voice* directed me.

While I can't say for certain that I can feel the higher frequencies that are present in the stones that adorn my fingers, I can attest that the synchronicities associated with living at a higher frequency significantly sped up around the time I purchased my tenth ring.

My business income increased exponentially as the amount of effort I expended in my business proportionally decreased. New people and experiences simply materialized. Twice in business deals I was bumped from being last to being first in position as if by divine intervention. Creative ideas that would never have occurred to me prior to wearing the rings popped into my head like they had been there forever. New team members appeared at the precise moment that their skills were needed to complete and publish *Just Say YES*.

I have significantly relaxed as I work in the unknown of each day. My *Inner* Voice communication is more clear and consistent than ever before. I no longer feel the need to control a person or an experience. Rather, I allow them to be revealed to me. Additional and more advanced reading material continues to flow to me that activates me to step into higher frequencies and new experiences.

I'm not saying that the energy field around my hands is strong enough to light my apartment if the electricity goes out. But I am grateful for being even more *Consciously Aware* and for living at and sustaining a higher frequency that continues to pull me forward.

Reading Higher Vibrational Material May Not Result In Bejeweled Digits, But It Will Consistently Activate You To Explore Ideas And Experiences Specific To Your Path That Are Tied To The Higher Frequencies Of Your Dreams And Desires.

Chapter 22
Your Inner Voice and Outer Appearances

WHENEVER WE FIND OURSELVES considering the *Outer Appearances*, we can be assured that we are not connected to our *Inner Voice*. We are instead living *Above The Neck* in our *Thinking Mind*, without *Conscious Awareness*, and where *Outer Appearances* rule supreme. Lacking *Inner Voice* guidance, we cannot find or maintain the higher frequencies tied to our *Highest Visions*; and more than likely, we are numb or blindly pursuing mere distractions. The truth is that *Outer Appearances* are really nothing more than false appearances that distract us from the deeper truth of our path.

In most cases, neither our parents nor our teachers learned to use their *Inner Voice* as a valuable life tool, depriving future generations of its vital gifts. Consequently, we too have lacked the knowledge of this vast resource.

Lacking inner guidance, high school and college students now face a critical time in their lives for which they are vastly unprepared to make career decisions, and in fact, may be held hostage by *Outer Appearances*. Chaos and massive emotional stress ensue as they blindly led by their *Thinking Mind* from *The Neck*, unaware that their *Inner Voice* is there to guide them to make those choices that are truest for their life's path.

Even graduated students who currently work in unfulfilling careers might well ask themselves if, upon tapping into their *Inner*

Voice, they can revisit their lives since graduation and see *NOW* what did not seem possible *THEN* when the *Outer Appearances* seemed insurmountable.

The truth for all of us is that it is never too late to connect with our Inner Voice.

Vast numbers within our society live *Above The Neck*, numbing themselves to the frustration of being disconnected from their inner wisdom. Subjecting themselves to the chaos of *Outer Appearances*, they distract themselves with overspending, serial dating, TV or overindulgence in sex, food, and liquor.

At whatever point you may be in your life, *NOW* is the time to recognize that *YOU* are responsible for *EVERYTHING* in your life.

Living from your *Inner Voice* causes a major shift in how the *Outer Appearances* appear to you, and in fact, they begin to fall away to reveal your truth. Yes, there are always bills to pay. Jobs to work. Kids to manage responsibly. But you will be operating within an energetic pull from a place of strength and love deep within yourself that will be your guide.

You will step away from the unconscious herd when you stop doing what no longer fits you. As you gain clarity, your *Inner Voice* will lead you to create a set of beliefs that are customized to support *YOU*. *Outer Appearances* will no longer have a stake in your daily decisions. Instead, they will merely serve to reflect back to you those issues or fears that you choose to release.

Personal Story
The Channeler

I recall far too many times when the *Outer Appearances* temporarily detained me on my journey as I fell prey to the chaos of my *Thinking Mind*. Failing to find resolution there, I would finally remember to go back down *Below The Neck* in search of my inner direction. Synchronicity would almost immediately ensue thereafter.

We are all blessed by those people we bring into our lives to help us look deeper inside ourselves. They are there to trigger us into a deeper *Conscious Awareness* through their presence, their words, their actions or a combination of sorts. In many cases, we know the truth in those moments, although our *Thinking Mind* likens them to holding a wiggling rattlesnake in a bag.

And so it was one afternoon when a woman, whom I had come to know casually on her frequent visits to my Montana restaurant, walked in. Her youngest son worked for me, and she and I had always maintained a casual friendship filled with engaging conversations.

She was quite striking with a beauty that at the time I did not realize emanated from within her. Her physical beauty only magnified the effect. Her life force, or aura, was off the charts, although I could not have understood this concept at the time since I was not as spiritually aware of, nor as connected to, my *Inner Voice*.

Which explains why I reacted the way I did, when one afternoon she looked me straight in the eye and told me that she had just returned from a spiritual workshop where she had worked with a Channeler, someone who can tune in to a plane other than the physical one in which we live and receive information useful to us. For the past month, she'd had this feeling that she should introduce me to this Channeler. She released a nervous giggle as she shared this information.

Her statement caught me completely off guard. I recall my entire body tightening up and my breath becoming shallow. Time appeared to stand still. Talk about triggered!

Above The Neck amidst the din in my *Thinking Mind*, I managed to respond to her in a clipped tone, "You definitely have the wrong guy because I don't even read my horoscope!"

Unfazed, she continued warmly, "Well, I have her number if you ever want it. You know where to reach me." She flashed that million-dollar smile, waved to junior, and off she went.

It wasn't until a few weeks later with more than a few nights spent facing my resistance within the chaos of my *Thinking Mind*, that I finally went *Below The Neck* and allowed my *Inner Voice* to tell me that her words had triggered a deeper knowing that I had been ignoring. Rather than facing it, I had been distracted by the *Outer Appearances of* a high-living lifestyle, social friendships, and the illusion of financial security.

The truth of my reality, however, was that I was bored with the restaurant, spiritually running on empty, deeply unhappy with my lack of personal growth, and unfulfilled with the life that I had worked for six years to create. Even worse, I didn't think I could stand to look at another taco without seeing a ball and chain tied to it. It was time for a change.

My *Inner Voice* told me exactly what I needed to do. I picked up the phone to dial my friend and ask for the introduction. The Channeler provided a session filled with information that changed my life. And with that, the next door opened, leaving six years of *Outer Appearances* lying in the snow outside.

Embrace Those Situations That Are Vitally Important And Divinely Necessary To Blow A Hole In Your Boat Filled With Outer Appearances, Forcing You To Get Out And Swim.

Chapter 23
Your Inner Voice *and Someone Else's Rules*

*S*OMEONE ELSE'S RULES OFFER opportunities for us to take action that brings us closer to *Who We Are* and *What We Came Here To Do*. Our *Inner Voice* makes us aware of the resistance we may have to taking that action.

Someone Else's Rules do not feel true to us, as though they violate some inner knowing we have. They also may reflect a personality behind the rules with which we feel uncomfortable. In many instances, *Someone Else's Rules* will cause us to expand past our comfort zone as we work to liberate ourselves from their influence.

Whatever they reflect to us, we may resist *Someone Else's Rules* by shutting down and becoming unconscious. Or by reacting in anger and frustration and feeling controlled and manipulated. Or by acting the role of a victim as though we've no choice in the matter. In all instances, we are resisting the need to be being *Consciously Aware* and move forward.

Yet *Someone Else's Rules* are really a two-fold blessing as they activate our *Inner Voice* to either (1) tell us that we are headed in a direction that feels true for us, or (2) trigger us to face the fact that those choices are no longer a fit for us. The gift they offer us is *Clarity*, as our *Inner Voice* directs us to move forward either way.

Far too many people are conditioned to follow *Someone Else's Rules* to feel safe, rather than embrace the truth that security exists only within us and not outside of us as the *Outer Appearances* falsely represent. They hate their jobs (or a situation), complaining or feeling victimized, instead of taking action toward a new career (or resolution). They are unwilling to take responsibility in the form of *Inner Voice*-directed action that could otherwise lead them away from where they don't want to be.

Someone Else's Rules apply to career professionals who follow a specific path (medical, law, finance), which pace and demand offer little chance for them to connect to their *Inner Voice* and create a structure for its practice and development. They voice frustration that they feel unfulfilled. Or wish they had room for the stretch of new experiences, and perhaps, that they had chosen a totally different path.

Even after they retire, they may fail to hear the calls of their Inner *Voice* having lived their entire lives in their *Thinking Minds* and tuned only into the *Outer Appearances*.

Military careers are similarly constrained by *Someone Else's Rules* due to the rigid boundaries (that are required) and conditions experienced by those who join its ranks. Those considering a military career would be better prepared to choose this path if they first learn to hear, trust, and act on their *Inner Voice* direction to know that it is a true fit for them as it can be for many.

Many of our service men and women who serve our country are, in fact, left stranded (and feel abandoned) when they finish their tour of duty. There is no *Inner Voice* education in place to help them create their *Personal Rules* as they reintegrate into non-military careers, where they are unaccustomed to the lack of *Someone Else's Rules* to guide them.

Be especially aware of *Someone Else's Rules* governing those individuals in whom you are encouraged to entrust authority. Do not discount your *Inner Voice's* resistance to professional advice that doesn't feel right to you. Don't allow someone with more education than you try to bulldoze what you know to be true inside! Follow your *Inner Voice's* guidance.

Regardless of why we have been living by *Someone Else's Rules*, *NOW* is the time to recognize that we are the ones who have allowed the rules to keep us from our passions, dreams, and personal expression in so many areas.

We may never have been taught to make creative expression a

priority in our lives. Nor were we taught to trust ourselves from inside out. Regardless, it is our responsibility to make our *Inner Voice* a priority if we are going to create the life that best reflects our personal truth.

Personal Story
Singing at the College National Finals Rodeo

Especially in my earlier years, I was not always *Consciously Aware* enough to act consistently on my *Inner Voice's* guidance. My *Thinking Mind* insisted it be dealt into the daily decisions and career plans I made, including my decision to become a singer after I sold my restaurant. "After all," it thought from *Above The Neck*, "I have a good voice and years of vocal training to support me!"

My *Thinking Mind* just knew that it could *Connect The Dots* to achieve my goal by booking a singing gig at the College National Finals Rodeo held in the same town where my restaurant had been located. Using my connections, I could secure a singing contract at the rodeo venue; and butta bing butta boom, I would soon croon to thousands of rodeo fans on my way to an overnight success story!

I booked the gig. I would open the rodeo finals singing the *Star Spangled Banner* and perform several other songs that evening, followed by two additional evenings of performances. I was on my way!

It came together so easily that at the time I might have thought it was my *Inner Voice* running the show. However, at the time I was still unaware of the term and of the power of its guidance, other than a few key moments when it had previously surfaced along my path.

The debacle that followed serves as an excellent example of where we can confuse circumstances *Above The Neck* where our *Thinking Mind Connects The Dots* with the true flow *Below The Neck* where our *Inner Voice* guides us each step of the way.

The day before my debut, the leader of the band (hired by the rodeo venue) told me that there was no time to rehearse our set. While I experienced an immediate inner knowing that this was unacceptable, I wasn't tuned in enough to my fledgling *Inner Voice* to hear and act on its guidance to stand up to *Someone Else's*

Rules. Instead, my *Thinking Mind* simply rationalized that everything would work out. Hadn't it been easy thus far?

The next evening as the band played the opening notes, I began to sing the National Anthem standing on a dais in the arena gazing out at ten thousand people with hands on hearts and eyes on the flag. The first few words rang out from me in perfect timing to the band's accompaniment… until *THAT* moment when I realized I had no clue where they were in the music.

And so I stopped singing.

And the band kept playing.

And I found myself staring out at ten thousand people who had turned their gaze from our nation's flag to stare back at me.

For what seemed to be an infinite number of agonizing moments, we stared at each other until the band played out the last notes.

I descended from the dais and walked across the arena and out of the gate never to return. It was the longest walk of shame that I have ever known.

I was fired the next day from the rest of the engagement.

So much for *Connecting The Dots*.

For years afterwards, the hair on the back of my neck would stand up whenever my *Thinking Mind* looked back to that night. It was the last, super ego fueled circumstance that it ever orchestrated. Even *IT* knows it doesn't like to live through epic failure!

When *Someone Else's Rules* don't work for you, let your *Inner Voice* do the talking. Had I been more deeply rooted in its wisdom, I would never have accepted the "No" that I could not rehearse the entire set before the performance. My *Inner Voice* knew I needed a rehearsal, but that inner knowing was trumped by my *Thinking Mind's* need to *Connect The Dots*, adhere to *Someone Else's Rules*, and rationalize that all was well in the *Outer Appearances*. Never again!

Your Inner Voice Will Help You To Create The Personal Rules That You Need To Walk Your Truest Path.

Chapter 24
Your **Inner Voice** *is God Within You*

TOO MANY PEOPLE DON'T like to hear the word "God." For many years, I was one of them. Youthful experiences tied to that three-letter word can be so painful that they go numb when God's name is invoked. I certainly don't judge them on it, especially since I no longer live in my *Thinking Mind*.

I encourage you, if you find yourself in that place, to *Just-Say-Yes* and transition past the pain you carry from *Someone Else's Rules* about God that were pushed on you earlier in your life. Trust your *Inner Voice* to guide you toward the spiritual practice and reading material that best works for you at this stage in your journey.

Experiences when God is pushed on you may seem all too familiar. A neighbor praises God during a play date with their child or never misses a chance to quote the Bible across the fence. Your coworker tells you indignantly that her God is the real one. Your parent used the specter of God's wrath to control you as a child.

Even using terms like "New Age" and "spiritual" in light conversation may result in righteous anger from those who judge your beliefs as being out of alignment with theirs.

The great news (Thank God!) is that you now trust yourself to make your decisions through your *Inner Voice*. Consequently, you are free to choose a name for God that is a fit for you. This is your truth!

There are infinite possibilities including, but certainly not limited to: *Higher Power, Source, Creator, Guide, Angel, Ascended Master, Higher Self, God Self, Divine Mind, I AM, Invisible Assistance, Higher Guidance, Highest Good,* or *Best Friend*. The energy associated with any one of these labels is the same; it is an awareness of a connection to higher assistance.

The more I trust my *Inner Voice* to lead me, the more *Consciously Aware* I am that I have always had higher assistance to help me connect to what I want in my life. Years passed before I fully cleansed myself of the rigid views that were imposed upon me by *Someone Else's Rules* about God in my youth.

My goodness, there certainly are a plethora of God-minded folk who can spout passages from their holy book, but who live wholly in their *Thinking Mind* full of judgment!

Personal Story
Singing in Church

One week on college break, my mother approached me (yet again) with her sales pitch that I should sing in church at the upcoming Sunday service. I was surprised given that I had made it as abundantly clear to her as it was clear to me (*Below The Neck*) that singing in front of HER PEOPLE was definitely not one of MY DESIRES. However, when her pitch turned to the plea, "But we never get to hear you sing anymore!" my *Thinking Mind* caved in.

I did stand my ground on one point in our negotiation. My good friend (who was also well liked by my family) would accompany me on the piano in lieu of the church pianist, who at times was so heavy handed on the ivories and who often times lagged so far behind the vocalist that I wondered if she'd gone home to God and her fingers were the only thing still in this dimension.

Thrilled at her successful negotiation, my mother flew to the phone to share the wondrous news with the minister that her son would be singing in church that Sunday. At the mention of my friend accompanying me, however, I watched her face contort. Her mouth dropped open and her brow furrowed (never a good sign) as the minister told her in no uncertain terms that he could not have my friend play the piano because she went to another church. And

THAT conflicted with *HIS* religious (and apparently God's) convictions!

My mother was stunned. The minister of *HER* church (my folks were founding members) was telling her that God didn't want our family friend to play the piano because she attended a different church? I inwardly wondered if my friend knew that she could now add the word "sinner" to her resume!

That phone call was a shock to my mother's system, especially since we had so many close friends and neighbors of various faiths. Driving my point home that her pastor's position was a perfect example of why I had never wanted to pass over the threshold of *HIS* house, I made it clear to her that God's right hand man had missed a golden opportunity to make a convert of my friend. I pictured her sitting trapped in the front pew, silently enduring his forty-five minute sermon, as the wind passed over his vocal cords directly into her face. I likened it to sitting directly in front of a fan with the speed set to *WAY* too high!

Needless to say, I did not sing in church that Sunday. Nor did my mother ever ask me to attend church again.

I believe in that moment on the phone with the pastor, my mother felt a shift within her as her *Inner Voice* revealed the cracks in the rigid dogma of *Someone Else's Rules* that no longer fit her.

As You Connect To Your* Inner Voice, *You Connect To Higher Assistance. Name It Anything You Want. Never Again Will You Question Its Place In Your Life As You Revel In Its Strength.

Chapter 25
Speaking from Your **Inner Voice**

THERE ARE TIMES WHEN I speak with someone, and for a time afterword, I remain filled with the *Inner Voice* energy that came up through me during the conversation. The current is so strong that it can feel like I am plugged into an electrical outlet. As I speak, I become aware of this powerful frequency that spreads through all parts of my body.

The other day I called a friend to ask a question. Early into the conversation, I became aware of a higher energetic frequency rooted in my *Inner Voice* that came through my speaking voice as I started to share what I knew/felt my friend needed to hear. It is similar to speaking with passion, but it has a different feel and energy that carries a ring of truth in the center of the message. I also became aware of a shift within my friend as she heard the truth in the message and felt its energetic pull.

Speaking-voice energy that emanates from your *Inner Voice* is not used to persuade someone to agree with you. Rather, it is so firmly rooted in your truth that, like it or not, your subject will hear the insightful information as it comes from that higher source, passing through you and out of your mouth. The information is always based in truth and it is what they are ready to hear, whether they are aware of it or not. You are merely the conduit.

And yes, at times the message is for you to hear for your own good too. What's most exhilarating about this level of energy flow is that at times you will suddenly feel inspired in your life by a truthful idea that you find yourself sharing with another person in conversation.

Once you are in the flow of this speaking-voice energy, you are no longer aware of being tired, hungry, on a tight schedule, or of any other personal needs. In most instances, you are only partially aware of what you are saying. At times your *Thinking Mind* may even have to play catch up with conversation! Time stands still, and the moment is only about the truth of the message being delivered.

It is not so much the tenor or volume of your voice as it is the frequency tied to what you say. People simply feel this energy as it activates them on some level, regardless of whether it appears to register with them. It is of no concern to you how or what they hear from you. That would otherwise be your *Thinking Mind* stepping in to judge their reaction. No. Stay *Below The Neck* in these moments.

Remember that when speaking from your *Inner Voice* with another, your *Thinking Mind* plays no role; you are *NOT* the doer, only a vessel. The message should be delivered with absolute and unconditional love and not from ego or with expectation of any outcome.

From this same place that has guided you *first* to your truth, you will also receive guidance to offer assistance to activate and awaken someone else to their truth. What a wondrous feeling we experience in these moments!

Personal Story
Hauling Straw Bales

While it would be several years from the age of seventeen before I would recognize and truly understand the words "*Inner Voice*," I nonetheless felt it grow stronger in my daily life even then. I felt it both within me and in the manner I came to speak with my family and with strangers around me. At times it seemed I was speaking from a deeper place of which I was unaccustomed and, in many instances, completely unaware.

One afternoon my brother and I were hauling truckloads of straw bales that Dad had sold to one of our neighbors. Five years my senior, my brother always tried to run the show according to his personal schedule; in this case, dictating to me that we should add an additional tier of bales per load that we were to haul that day. Driven purely by his *Thinking Mind* to finish more quickly that day, perhaps to impress Dad, he recklessly disregarded Dad's instructions on the amount of bales per load that we could safely haul.

Consequently, my brother overloaded the bales on the truck despite my protestations. I felt/knew that we were headed for trouble. As we approached a hill, I gently reminded him that we should at least keep the truck to the center of the road so it didn't lean and lose part of our load down over the bank. But you couldn't tell him anything. Certainly, my seventeen years of experience on this earth was of no value to him, so my repeated warning of the danger ahead went unheeded.

And then it happened. We took the curve too sharply and lost a big chunk of bales off the side of the load and down over a steep bank. As we walked back to peer over the edge, I saw that many of the bales were stopped by a fence that clung to the hillside. What a mess. And then my brother uttered the words that awakened a new level of my *Inner Voice*. He told me that *WE* had better get started hauling the bales up over the bank!

It seemed in that moment that time stood still. In reaction to his barked orders, my *Inner Voice* suddenly and powerfully activated as though it had been lifting weights for years and never tested its strength. I responded to him in such a manner and in such clarity that I think it shocked both of us. In that moment of speaking *MY* inner truth, my brother became aware of a power in me he'd never experienced, even as I became aware of it myself. As I came to understand later, it had been growing within me all those years.

My *Inner Voice* told him, in no uncertain terms, that he was now going to take full responsibility for his willful decisions and disregard of my warnings. It continued to inform him that *HE* was going to haul every bale up that bank by himself. Finally, I heard myself telling him that I was walking back to the closest neighbor, calling Mom to come get me, and then I was going to drive into town and see a movie!

Even as he jumped around, cursing and yelling at me to get back there, we both knew that things had changed forever between us. My speaking-voice energy had never been stronger than in those moments, and my words had never been so eloquent. I laughed as I walked away thinking he shouldn't be wasting his energy jumping around and yelling with the mess he had to clean up.

When I recounted the situation to my parents, they heard the shift in me too, and the three of us had a good laugh at my brother's comeuppance.

Until that moment, I had no idea the impact that speaking-voice energy from my *Inner Voice* would have on another person until it flexed its power within me that afternoon. The voice inside me was strong enough to stand up to the unconscious (and outrageous) behavior based upon *Someone Else's Rules*.

My *Inner Voice* taught me that I was strong enough to speak my truth and no longer tolerate or accept my brother's behavior. It was indeed a defining moment in my life. And I suppose my brother's life as well.

Speaking From Our* Inner Voice *Conveys Our Deepest Truths And Activates The Truths Within Those To Whom We Speak.

Chapter 26
Your Inner Voice is Your Personal GPS

IN AN EARLIER CHAPTER, I mentioned that working with your *Inner Voice* and frequency is like moving up and down the radio dial and tuning into different stations. You can't see the radio frequencies, and yet you know that something must be there to carry the music that you can hear. When you place your coffee cup in the microwave, you don't see the microwaves at work, yet after a minute or so your coffee emerges piping hot.

Inner Voice energy works the same way. I can't see the energy connected to it any more than I can see a radio frequency or a microwave. But I feel the energy as it pulls/pushes me, and I enjoy tangible results when I honor it.

It is my *Personal GPS*, a radar guidance system that is specific to my life path.

Are you ready to stop resisting what you can't see? Consider the 'Dark Night of The Soul' situations that many of you may face at some point in your life when you feel overwhelmed by credit card debt; are unemployed and can't find a job; or feel alone with no one to love.

These are the watershed moments when you face a fork in your road. Are you willing to finally go *Below The Neck* and allow your *Inner Voice* to serve as your *Personal GPS* to show you the way out of your current situation? Even though you can't see it and may not yet even be able to feel it?

If you find yourself resisting as you read this, you are still *Above The Neck* in your *Thinking Mind*. Our *Thinking Mind* resistance tells us that it doesn't exist if we can't See it! Touch it! Hear it! Or that it is not real if it isn't instant gratification! How easily we forget that our troubled situations took months or years to accrue, and yet we expect instant relief!

Resistance goes hand in hand with anything new and unfamiliar. We won't try a new dessert that tastes different or wear a new shade of purple shirt that we were attracted to on the rack. Or break our routine. Our *Thinking Mind* is still running the show. Now is when we can choose to go inside and look to our *Personal GPS* for help. But first we have to *Just—Say—Yes*!

Working *Below The Neck* and *Above The Waist*, you no longer allow your *Thinking Mind* to tell you that it will take five years to pay off the credit cards. Or worry about the 'How Tos' of your job search. Or whether you will find a partner. Or that you must plan before you act. You will never again have to ask Who, What, Where, When, How, or Why. These are all terms used by the *Thinking Mind* to distract you from relying on your *Personal GPS*.

Just—Say—Yes, and stop resisting challenges by over thinking or ignoring them. By looking at them. By complaining about them. Don't allow your *Thinking Mind* to judge, edit, or control your actions. Instead, hear, trust, and act on your *Inner Voice* guidance.

Just—Say—Yes, and call the credit card companies to acknowledge the debt and set up the minimum payment plan, trusting that your inner guidance will lead you toward the solution that works for you.

Just—Say—Yes, and search the Internet for the job categories that interest you. Share with your friends, family, or strangers the information describing the job that you want.

Just—Say—Yes, and sign-up for an on-line dating site. Sign up for more than one. Write out a profile of *Who You Are* and *Who Your Mate Is*.

Just—Say—Yes, and in that moment, you will cross over that invisible line of resistance.

Trust that your *Personal GPS* will pull you forward as your life opens up in front of you when you begin to *Just-Say-Yes* in all areas of your life. Your *Inner Voice* has all the strength, love, and power to support you. Trust the divine radar guidance system that is your *Personal GPS*.

There were many days that all I could do was *Just-Say–Yes* to my *Highest Vision* for this book and then sit down at the computer to face my *Thinking Mind's* resistance. In every instance, it simply evaporated. It will for you too.

Personal Story
Trusting My Personal GPS

The morning that I felt inexplicably pulled to drop my college classes, put on my ski clothes, and hop in the car for the drive up to the ski hill, I chose to honor the pull of my *Personal GPS*.

In those early days, I skied mogul after mogul as my *Personal GPS* pulled me forward in the direction of *Who I Am* and *What I Came Here To Do*. I fluctuated daily between *Below The Neck* elation and *Above The Neck* dread as my radar guidance system led me further away from the herd mentality of my classmates. I saw them in the evenings and regaled them with my day's adventures, but I could not share with them the turmoil that I felt inside. I had never known such a solitary existence.

In sub-zero temperatures, I skied daily, alone, in the chaos of my *Thinking Mind's* confusion and self-doubt. What would I tell my father? What would I do for money when it ran out? What was I thinking? My bumps and spills seemed to shake up feelings of paralyzing fear and overwhelming guilt that surfaced up into my *Thinking Mind*.

Yet in time, I learned to trust the feeling of my *Inner Voice's* pull. I felt its power growing inside of me as I was led in a direction away from the chaos and fear of my *Thinking Mind* as it considered the *Outer Appearances*. Although I was not then aware of it, this inner power and the freedom that appeared with it (and no homework!) was part of my *Personal GPS*-directed road map. It was programmed and locked on to my future *Highest Visions*.

Throughout that semester, I never once considered going back to class, thanks to the support of my *Personal GPS*. All these years later, it has pulled me right up to writing these pages in anticipation of sharing my *Inner Voice* journey with you.

That Winter Alone On The Hill, My* Personal GPS *Guided Me In A Direction That Was The Truest Fit For Who I Am and What I Came Here To Do.

Chapter 27
Your Inner Voice *and* Living in the Abundance Flow

FOLLOWING YOUR *INNER VOICE'S* guidance will provide you with an *Abundance Flow* with which you are matched in frequency at any given moment. When I speak of *Abundance Flow*, I mean timing, relationships, connections, introductions, and personal shifts, in addition to financial abundance, that are integral parts of a greater divine web of synchronicity.

Abundance Flow is part of the greater whole that is *You* working at all levels within yourself and with your surrounding environment. It includes personal growth, raised *Conscious Awareness* and the inner clarity that *You* can accept the *Who You Are* that best reflects the abundance that you seek to attract.

As you hear, trust and act on your *Inner Voice's* guidance, you will gain a sense of how it feels to be in the pull of *Abundance Flow*. Part of the *Abundance Flow* actually lies *within* this process. The more you fully trust your *Inner Voice's* guidance, the more *Abundance Flow* you will experience.

The more I have come to hear, trust and act on my *Inner Voice's* guidance, the closer I have also come to the edge of my comfort zone where my *Thinking Mind* cannot begin to plan when, where and how my *Abundance Flow* will appear. In fact, I learned years ago to simply let go of my *Thinking Mind's* expectations or need to *Connect The Dots*.

I have come to understand and accept that I am not the doer in my life. Rather, I am simply following my *Inner Voice's* directions, and in my experience of *Abundance Flow*, the bills get paid as I continue to achieve my *Highest Visions*.

While everything works out in divine timing, I have also come to understand that the outcome has nothing to do with the process, much less my asserting control over it. Nor does the outcome always resemble any expectations my *Thinking Mind* might anticipate. Rather, I fully trust and accept that my *Inner Voice* has led me through a process and to an outcome that is divinely intended as my *Abundance Flow*.

For example, you may feel that being debt-free is the *Abundance Flow* that you seek. If you are working only from your *Thinking Mind*, your desire to be debt-free may simply be a need that originated as the result of past guilt or pain connected to old spending patterns or being controlled by someone who held the purse strings. You may perceive that being debt-free will make you happy. In all these instances, your *Thinking Mind* is focused solely on *Outer Appearances*.

Until you drop *Below The Neck* to work with your *Inner Voice*, however, you may never realize that being debt-free may not truly reflect *Who You Are*. Nor may it reflect *Who You Are* with respect to your *Highest Visions*. I have several relatives and acquaintances that have no debt *AND* no sense of *Who They Are* or *What They Came Here To Do*. In fact, they are miserable most of the time in their debt-free lives.

Abundance Flow that is tied to your *Inner Voice's* guidance may be either debt-free living or living with high, manageable stress-free debt. In either case, it will be abundance that truly reflects *Who You Are* and *What You Came Here To Do*.

Personal Story
Earnest Money or Dental Work

When I made an offer to purchase my first house, my real estate broker (who was also a spiritually-inclined friend) knew that I didn't have all of the earnest money deposit in my bank account when I submitted the offer to the Seller. Acting in her professional capacity, she felt obligated to go *Above The Neck* and speak to me.

She sternly said, "This is serious because this contract is a legal document."

Being clear that I was acting from my *Inner Voice's* guidance, however, I told her to proceed with submitting the offer. And then we waited. No response from the seller for months.

Yet over those months I lived within an *Abundance Flow* that I knew was tied to the house purchase. Guided by my *Inner Voice* at every step, I knew that the money was all there for the closing. By the time the contract was accepted and the closing date was set, I had the full amount of the earnest money deposit physically in my account.

Then a month before closing I was faced with an emergency (as in unexpected) dental work that took half of my accumulated deposit. I fully admit that I became tense as I jumped into my *Thinking Mind*. However, I had made the offer as a result of my *Inner Voice's* direction, and it continued to feel true for me, so I just quickly dropped back down *Below The Neck* and trusted in continued *Abundance Flow*.

A week or so after the dental work, I was visiting on the phone with a friend that I hadn't seen for some time. During our conversation I happened to mention my unexpected dental bills since we both have many capped teeth and she completely understands the expense of undergoing the work. Without any prompting by me, or any mention of the scheduled house closing in our discussion, she suddenly said, "I just sold my apartment. Do you need a loan for your upcoming closing? I'm happy to do it!" And here was the *Abundance Flow* tied to the house closing and divinely guided by my *Inner Voice*!

As with this experience, I have come to understand that invoices are always paid in divine time on those purchases that are tied to commitments that I make when I act on my *Inner Voice's* guidance. In this instance, my *Abundance Flow* supplied me with additional funds to pay the loan back soon after the closing, and with interest that my friend hadn't required or expected.

Your Abundance Flow Is Directly Tied To The Frequency Of Who You Are With Respect To The Frequency Of That Abundance.

Epilogue

*J*UST SAY YES HAS activated you to trust yourself *Below The Neck And Above The Waist* to live from your *Inner Voice's* guidance. You are now, in essence, "out" of your *Thinking Mind* and living in the flow of your *Inner Voice*. You are closer to discovering *Who You Are* and *What You Came Here To Do*.

As you relax into this inner process, you will begin to feel/know that life challenges big or small will be handled. Your *Thinking Mind* will be aware of this feeling and it will remain calm and connected to this inner sense without need to override it or *Connect The Dots*.

You will no longer feel angst as you face the *Vast Unknown*. You will no longer feel lost and hopeless, or overwhelmed and confused. You will instead continue to expand your *Conscious Aware*ness of all that is true for you, bringing new and enriching experiences into your life.

My next book, *Conscious Desire,* introduces you to three concepts that are not recognized in the physical world and that can't be rationally explained, but about which you will become more *Consciously Aware* having read *Just Say YES: Energy Cords, Soul Contracts* and *Soul Pulses*. The book's title reflects the point that you can't manifest what is true for you until you become more *Consciously Aware* of your desires *(ie: Highest Visions)*.

You achieve this awareness in part through hearing, trusting and acting on your *Inner Voice's* guidance. This awareness is further strengthened through the *Energy Cords* that bump you. As you come to discover your *Soul Contract,* you will also become more aware of the underlying daily pull of your *Soul Pulse.*

Energy Cords

Energy Cords are links of energy between your *Inner Voice* and everything else around you.

When you feel drawn or attracted to something, there is an *Energy Cord* stretching between you and that item to which you feel strongly pulled. Tapping into that forward pull and utilizing your *Inner Voice* will bring a stronger awareness and clarity to your day.

Whether *Energy Cords* are active or dormant, they work as vibrational compasses. They contain all the divine abundance, divine scheduling, divine direction, divine process, and divine unfolding to lead you forward. They will help you to manifest all that you want in your life because they resonate with the deepest part of *Who You Are* and *What You Came Here To Do.*

Soul Contracts

Now stay with me here! I have introduced you to the concept of *Energy Cords*. Are you ready for more? Remember that each of you can be every bit the explorer like Lewis & Clark.

A *Soul Contract* is an agreement that you (your Soul) signs on a spiritual dotted line before you manifest into the physical 3D world. You have chosen certain family groups and interactions with other Souls in your Soul Group to create learning experiences in this lifetime that are part of your Soul Contract.

You have chosen to be on the earth at this specific time. Wow! You chose to go on your Lewis & Clark trek during this time of great change! Oh boy do we need you! Thank you for being here to help.

Soul Pulse

Your *Soul Pulse* is the underlying pull that has been with you every day of your life and that helps you to better understand your *Soul Contract*. It is the energy that underlies *Who You Are* and *What You Came Here To Do.*

Soul Pulse energy is different from the energy bumping you from *Energy Cords* or your *Inner Voice* energy coming up through you and into your *Thinking Mind*. It is a subtle, smooth energy that completely bypasses your *Thinking Mind* and bypasses your *Conscious Awareness*, yet still causes you to act before your *Thinking Mind* is aware of it.

The distinction is that *Energy Cord and Inner Voice* energies further raise your awareness of the flow your *Soul Pulse* energy. Through the use of all three of these energies, you will have now shifted enough to be more aware of the subtle but powerful energy of your *Soul Contract*.

Conclusion

You and I may not face Lewis & Clark's physical challenges as they explored the vast western frontier. We are, however, inner explorers who face the last great frontier within each of us.

We can no longer be sleepers. We face a critical point on this planet as we do in our inner development. We must decide if we are willing to raise our *Conscious Awareness* to better confront our global and inner challenges. We must set out *NOW* into the *Vast Unknown* within us. There are valuable gifts inside each of us that the world needs.

Just Say YES has prepared you to be *Consciously Aware* of what is resonating within you! So are you going to saddle the horse or just watch the rodeo? Are you on the sidelines or are you in the game? *Just—Say—Yes* to *YOU*!

Hear, Trust, And Act On Your Inner Voice *Guidance As You Stand In The Light Of Who You Are and What You Came Here To Do.*

Visit www.ErecLindberg.com *to learn more about the* Inner Voice *journey, find Erec's suggestions for additional* Inner Voice-*related material, and to share your personal experiences. Be sure to register to receive a special notice when* Conscious Desire *is released!*

Join your fellow Inner Voice enthusiasts at **Say Yes To Your Inner Voice,** *an interactive blog where Erec shares his Inner Voice-directed thoughts.*

Contact Erec at info@ereclindberg.com *if you are interested in* Inner Voice-*directed* **Coaching Sessions**.

Made in the USA
Middletown, DE
10 January 2015